Embracing Your WILD Feminine

JOY MOATES

EMBRACING YOUR WILD FEMININE

Copyright © 2020 by Joy Moates

All rights reserved. Printed in the United States of America. No part of this book may be used or reproduced in any manner whatsoever without written permission except in the case of brief quotations embodied in critical articles or reviews.

Published by Words of Passion, Atlanta, GA 30097.

Cover Art: Joy Moates
Editorial: Nanette Littlestone
Cover Layout and Interior Design: Peter Hildebrandt

ISBN: 978-0-9996579-8-0 (paperback)
ISBN: 978-0-9996579-9-7 (e-book)

For Leah,
my daughter,
who is her own beautiful wild feminine spirit
and

Johnny
Our wild passion is my muse

Contents

1. Embrace Your Wild, Feminine Nature 5
   - Shakti—our feminine energy 10
   - The core feelings of your wild feminine are desire, joy, gratitude, freedom, abundance, creativity, sex, and sensuality. 11
   - How has embracing my wild feminine energy—my wild softness— enriched my life? 15
   - Feeling into this moment 17

2. The Journey with My Wild Feminine Spirit. 19
   - Using our bodies for meditation 25
   - Opening your heart 31
   - Journaling prompts for you 32

3. Who Are You? 35
   - Meditation—who am I? 37
   - A nourishing meditation 38
   - Guided imagery meditation—your free spirit. 42

4. Presence. 45
   - A practice for each day—wonder. 56
   - A deeper embodied meditation 58

5. Knowing Our Bodies as Our Home. 63

6. The Feminine Power of Receiving. 69
   - Short meditation for receiving 75

7. Gratitude and Abundance 79

8. Everyday Magic. 91
   - You are the magic. 92
   - Finding our magic meditation 94

9. Everyday Creativity 97
   Drawing/Painting—bringing out the Picasso in you! 106
   Writing 108

10. Wild Bodies/Moving Our Bodies 113
    A movement embodiment exercise 118
    Start your day with movement/My practice 121

11. Rituals—Daily Simple Ways to Connect with Your
    Inner Wildness 125
    Coffee ritual 127
    Morning meditation and gentle movement—ritual 129
    Morning blessing or devotional 131
    Morning blessing 132
    Another morning blessing 132
    Bedtime ritual 133
    Evening blessing 133
    Another evening blessing 134
    Tiny everyday rituals 134
    Essential oils 144

12. The Moon and Moon Cycles. 147
    New moon ritual example................................... 149
    Full moon ritual example 151

13. Pleasure and Desire 155
    Desire 156
    Journaling prompts 159
    Pleasure 161
    Journaling prompts 165
    Sensual embodied movement practice for your hips and pelvis . 167

14. Sensuality.................................... 171
    Journaling prompts 174
    A journaling practice for sensuality 177

15.	**Sexuality and Pleasure** 179
	Sensual body meditation practice—loving your body........... 185
	Nude body embodiment and love meditation 191
	Movement exercise—releasing your pelvic floor for pleasure ... 198
	Sex as mindfulness... 202
	Relaxing blissful breath 204
	Re-sensitizing our bodies................................... 205
	Orgasmic breathing 207
16.	**Eroticism** 211
	Meditation: Erotic merging of our inner feminine with our inner masculine (Sensual balancing of our Shiva and Shakti) 216
17.	**Nourishing and Nurturing Our Wild Feminine Bodies** 221
	Being nude—and feeling at home in your body 222
	Some easy self-care practices for getting in touch with and falling in love with your body 224
18.	**Holding All Our Emotions**..................... 229
	Making everything sacred especially during scary times......... 237
	Meditation—the power we do have in troubled times 240
	Wild feminine is (to me) 245
	Juicy.. 248

Conclusion 251
Journal prompts 253

Acknowledgments................................265

Additional Resources 267
Meditations 267

▼

I am wild, fierce, and holy
I am the divine feminine
I am a lover, creator, wild woman, soft companion, mother, daughter

I cherish and nourish my body
I let the soft animal of my body love what it loves
I embrace fully and own my sensuality and sexuality
in my bones I know my sexual energy is my life force, my creativity,
my ability to live juicy and deep and sweet

> Eros is my lover
> Life is my lover

with my wild feminine energy, I feel and touch my world
and with this energy I open myself to be touched by my world
I embrace my humanness, my wild spirit
I embody joy, sensuality, gratitude, and, most of all, love

can you hear her?
here, right now
take a deep full breath
here . . . what do you feel?
breathe deeper
open a little more
can you hear her whispering softly?
a gentle rhythm in your belly
here . . . drop deeper . . . listen
she offers peace and passion
gentle flows and turbulent waters
moon-filled nights and dark shadows
She is Life, She is You

passion,
you've been my lover
for years . . . I could not live without you
early, you taught me
how good it feels to be
fully absorbed
how to close my eyes
and just feel . . .
even if just my imagination

passion,
I feel you brush my skin, teasing
I feel your breath, your heartbeat
it always seduces me . . . I can't resist you
back to love, back to my muse
without you, passion, I am adrift
please don't leave me

when I answer your seduction
I am alive
I am free
I am whole

Chapter 1

Embrace Your Wild, Feminine Nature

"We're wild, with fire in our blood, wine in our bellies, and the moon in our souls."
– Oakthorne

Do you know your wild, feminine self? Do you live with her daily, or do you just have an idea that she lingers somewhere within you, maybe long forgotten?

Listen closely. Can you hear her whispers?

She is waiting for you to embrace her. As you embrace her, you free yourself. You will be real and raw and it feels oh so sweet.

You have a faint memory that tickles and scratches at your heart, but maybe you're not even quite sure what that niggling feeling is. It is your deeply buried feminine nature—your wildness—the ancient part of you. She has been with you since your first breath, just waiting to be re-awakened. We women are fierce, holy, and wild. We are cyclical beings with strong emotions. We are creators. Life emanates from us in so many ways. We may have forgotten that, but the pulse of our wild, holy selves still beats deep inside us and we can remember our unique true selves. And when we do that our spirits, our souls, our bodies feel as if they've taken a deep breath.

It feels so good, so rich, so peaceful. Embracing your wild, intuitive, feminine energy is your divine right. Honoring and embracing this beautiful, and sometimes chaotic, energy lets you live life to its fullest. Life is richer—passion, sensuality, and joy flow into your life.

The wild, intuitive feminine is a sexual creature, and she enjoys it. This sexual energy is your life force. She is full of the elements of nature—earth, fire, water, air, spirit, and especially the moon. This energy is your passion for all of life. It is your creativity, your gratitude, your love and compassion. It is your joy of life. This wild you is sensuous, she is sexual, a creator, a healer. She is authentic. She is passionate. She is wild and holy and fierce. The wild feminine is raw, never afraid of being messy, not afraid to be real, to be vulnerable, to be herself. She seeks pleasure in life and makes no apologies. She knows how to receive pleasure as well as give pleasure.

We live in a linear, get-it-done energy oriented world where that "always busy" mentality is revered: To-do lists, accomplishments, goals, striving, pushing. We all need that fire energy to get things done. Goals and accomplishments are excellent things—if they are meaningful. But it seems we've forgotten the ease, the receptivity, the heart-centeredness of our fierce, wild feminine. She is also full of fire, yet knows when to pause.

She is there, waiting for us. In fact, encouraging us to embrace her. When we open to her, allowing ourselves to feel everything we feel, no apologies, we discover our true selves. We begin to feel really juicy and alive. We feel sensuous, strong, yet open and vulnerable. We begin to live with a passionate, open heart. We see that we are perfect just as we are. Nothing to fix. Our imperfections and our messiness are holy.

The feelings that weave through our lives, our stories, as we embrace our wildness, are many and multi-faceted— passion, sexuality, sensuality, rawness, vulnerability, gratitude for it all, rage, sorrow. We know deep inside that all our emotions need to be welcomed, felt and honored.

We know to be truly wild, truly authentic, we need to feel viscerally. We need to know our darkness as well as our light, not to fix ourselves but to enrich our lives. Living as a wild, fierce, holy woman feels juicy, succulent, and untamed. In truth, it is acknowledging and embracing our humanness. What could be more right?

Do you remember how to feel? Or have you been suppressing your feelings so long that you don't even remember how or what you feel? If so, be gentle with yourself. It's okay.

Are you living your authentic life in this moment?

Or are you living the life you believe is expected of you?

Maybe these questions have brought sadness to your heart because you don't know yourself anymore. Or maybe you feel you're living an authentic life, but you just know, deep down in your belly, that there is more—more depth, more fullness, more deliciousness.

Answering the call of your wild feminine is a luscious journey, full of juicy woman-ness, sometimes an emotional roller coaster, but always culminating in a deep inner trust—trusting our bodies, our emotions. We trust the creation of our own lives. There are times we will be vulnerable and afraid, maybe often, but we know we are living from our sacred source—our belly and our heart. And we know we are sacred and wild. This is where we are supposed to live.

We desire to live life at our own pace, to find our freedom. We want to heal and thrive and love and hurt—to feel all of it deeply, no matter our age, no matter our circumstances. We desire to be authentic.

When you feel the ecstasy of passion and can also be brought to your knees in surrender and despair, you know you are truly alive, alive in all its depth, richness, pleasure and pain.

Say yes, even if right now it's only a whisper.

She's waiting. Your life will never be the same.

So if you're ready, if you're intrigued, listen to the seductive whispers of your wild self. She is smiling, playfully and seductively beckoning you to awaken. She knows how juicy and ripe and passionate you are.

Awakening and answering the call of your wild self brings you feelings of:

* Ease in your own skin
* Sensual and sexual pleasures, with or without a partner
* Being present and being held in this moment
* Abundance and gratitude for all of it
* Freedom—wild and delicious authenticity

You may ask yourself, how do I know my wild feminine self? You will feel her in your bones. She is wild, but not as in chaotic and crazy. She is ancient. She is primal. She is nature. She lives with and is the cycles of nature, cycles of the moon. She waxes and wanes. She manifests and she rests. She understands life itself is a cycle. She knows that movement is life. She is fluid and watery. Receptive but fierce. She is you before you were tamed by society. She is your true essence, the one that knows how to live with ease and flow through life. She is resilient and strong because she knows how to replenish her spirit.

In Tantra, the element of the Feminine is water. But our feminine wild self is also fire. Not the masculine fire of doing, but the fire of passion, desire, yearning, creating. She is the true fire of life. She is the fire in our bellies.

And this seemingly contradiction of elements—fire and water—is what makes her so powerful and why embracing her makes our lives so rich.

Our wild self is raw, brutally honest, yearning for pleasure, desirous of a meaningful life. She knows that the power of life joined with the fluidity of opening to receive is the way to all those desires. The way to a meaningful life. Her fire, as well as her fluidity, comes from the same place—her heart. Her love. This doesn't mean she never rages. Sometimes love has to destroy in order to create.

If this seems a little confusing, it is okay. One of our biggest lessons as we embrace our wildness is that we must live in the not-knowing. There will be periods of knowing and then often long periods of just trusting in the not-knowing. And you'll find that living in that trust of the not-knowing is a sweet place. A powerful place.

Shakti—our feminine energy

Shakti is a Sanskrit word embodying the female energy. It is the name of our feminine power. She is the energy that moves through everything. She is the energy that moves through us. She can be joy, anger, bliss, ecstasy. When we are in our Shakti, we are living in the present moment. We are in our bodies. We are receptive and open. When we drop into our feelings, into our bodies, we find our true power in this present moment. We embrace the energy that is moving through us. The passion that is moving through us. When we drop into this passionate energy, we can fully trust ourselves.

Shakti is also our sexual energy. This energy gives us creation—creation of everything. Sexual energy is not just about sex. That is an exquisite part of it, but sexual energy is so much more.

Without Shakti, we feel lackluster, dried-up, moving routinely through life. Our lives may be good, maybe we have many successes by society's standards, but we have no passion, no wonder. Maybe we don't feel anything deeply. We are seldom moved to tears or moans of passion—about anything.

The core feelings of your wild feminine are desire, joy, gratitude, freedom, abundance, creativity, sex, and sensuality.

In living from that place of wildness, you will feel ease and peace, rather than struggle and push. Just opening yourself up to receive, rather than always pushing, will change your life.

Our feminine nature is one of receptivity and our receptivity is what many of us have lost. We know how to give, to give until it hurts, but we don't know how to just receive what we need. And when we don't know how to receive, we also don't know how to ask for what we need. And to ask unapologetically.

How would it feel if, for just one day, you softened your body and your heart and just let what you need flow in? Wholeheartedly receiving. How good would that feel? It might feel a little scary, because it's not what you're used to doing. Moving out of our comfort zone is always scary but oh so necessary if we are to embrace our wildness.

It might also be a little scary because you may not even know what you wish to receive, what you need. You've lost touch with your body, your heart, your spirit. But with a little bit of delicious practice, you can come home to yourself. Remember who you are.

Breathe in and allow life to come to you. All that you desire, and deserve, is waiting for you. Just breathe it in and soften. Soften and feel your aliveness move through you. See how good it feels to open, to feel softness, to receive.

The practice of getting back in touch with your wildness is truly luscious and sweet. No arduous tasks. Just moments filled with touching, gentle exploring and questions, opening yourself up to feeling—little by little. I promise you will love it, even if it feels a little uncomfortable.

I write this to share with you some of the beliefs, rituals, etc. that work deliciously for me in hopes that some, or many, of them may benefit you. But I am not you, and you are not me. Every woman's journey is different and, most of all, embracing your wild feminine is about trusting yourself implicitly—your intuition, your inner voice and guidance, your wild deep knowing. That knowing is ancient and wise. It is beautiful.

So I desire to stir up questions and thoughts, ideas, so you can begin to find your own wild feminine path. So you can come home to yourself. Nothing else matters. We are extremely complicated beings and I don't believe we can condense anything into Steps 1, 2, and 3 that work for everyone. Our wild spirit just doesn't work that way.

I'll ask you questions and I'll tell you a little about me and what I have found brings me back and keeps me living from my wild spirit. I'll give you some of my rituals and meditations that will bring you into your body and into your spirit of receiving. It is my desire to share these practices and ideas with you, as woman to woman. As I tell my yoga students, you are your best teacher. Your body is your best teacher. So just open your heart, take in my words, maybe try some practices, and then choose what resonates with you. That way, you find the path perfect for you, back to your wild self. And I promise you that your path, as mine has, will be re-birthed many times and sometimes will just meander, because we are always evolving. And that is a wondrous thing.

You might want to have a journal to use just for this journey. One in which you can answer questions, free write, write your feelings after meditating. A place you can spill your heart and belly onto the page.

So read, browse, ponder, question, absorb. As you do this, see what resonates with you. Give it a try, take what feels right to you, and leave the rest. Truly. And when you take what resonates with you, feel free to change it in any way so that it feels just perfect for you. Everything, every act, on your journey to your wild self should feel exquisitely yours. And sometimes that tweaking takes place after you've practiced or absorbed the material (rituals, blessings, etc.) for a while and then you'll just know intuitively how to make it your own. And when meditating or saying blessings or intentions, your own words are so powerful. Because they are your own words, they resonate with your spirit, with your true desires. They are so much more than words. They are visceral. You feel them in your body. Remember, your thoughts are prayers, your words are spells (or intentions). So, so powerful. Yes, they are. Notice what you think. Be aware of the words you use.

As you find yourself remembering your wild feminine spirit, you will feel passionate and fiercely alive. You will feel at home in your body and know your body as your home. You will feel free and authentic. You will feel you are supported by grace in your life. Best of all, you will embrace your raw, messy self in all her beautiful glory.

So I invite you to sit with me. Imagine us sitting together on cushions, with a cup of coffee or tea, or a glass of wine, and let's share. Read slowly, ponder, "share" with yourself with my journal prompts. Enjoy and take great pleasure in re-uniting with your wild, holy self. See the twinkle and excitement in her eyes. Her eyes are your eyes.

Most of all, remember you are love. You are perfect just as you are. No fixing, just embracing.

How has embracing my wild feminine energy —my wild softness—enriched my life?

I have been a turned-on woman all of my life, but now, even in my later years, I am the most exquisitely turned on I have ever been. Because I have learned to fully embrace, and live from, my wild feminine. Oh, life is so passionate and juicy when I come from this sweetness and rawness. This is me being fully human—embracing my woman-ness, my wholeness, my holiness.

I have always embraced my sensuality and sexuality. I have had many delicious lovers. My life has been full of feeling. As I have fully embraced my wildness and set her free, over the past few years, the richness and sensuality of my life—that turned-on life force—has exponentially increased. My life began to flow with more ease and less worry. Pleasure became my way of life.

What does my wild self need and want? Deep pleasures. Pleasures that give meaning and fullness to my life. Pleasures felt through an open, vulnerable heart and body. I learned that the more I opened myself up to life and lovers and friends, and the more honest and vulnerable I was, the more life opened up to me. And, best of all, I could taste its richness.

Our wild feminine takes us deep into life, no longer just living on its surface. Yes, that means there are times I hurt deeply, but there are oh so many times that I am ecstatic, that I feel as if my heart is bursting open with all the goodness—almost too much to contain. It's exquisite.

Living from my wildness helps me be present in my body. When in my body fully, I notice things I might not have noticed before. I see and feel the magic that is around us all the time, the extraordinary that lies just beneath the ordinary.

There is always magic, and our wild softness sees that, feels it, magical creatures that we are. It is from embracing my wild feminine, that deep, sweet part of me, that I have found the magic, the magic in me and the magic in my world. Our world. All of us have that magic. Magic is something we are.

Why do I feel the wild feminine or the divine feminine is important? It has helped me to quit pushing and striving constantly. It has shown me that I will receive without near as much angst, pushing, and power. And actually the wild feminine is power, just power of a different nature. It is the power of receptivity, of allowing, of accepting, of loving, a power of ease and gratitude. It is the power of knowing and trusting that the universe supports me in so many ways. Wild feminine is the power of creating and manifesting through my desires and feelings.

The wild feminine has taught me to embrace fully my weirdness, my wildness, and it has helped me love myself even more. It taught me that I am a cyclical creature and an emotional creature, and that it is okay—not just okay but mandatory—that I caress and honor all my emotions and cycles.

I've lived most of my life by feeling, but because of my feminine practice, now more than ever, I soften more, desire more, make decisions from my heart and belly. I believe that the very beginning of the wild feminine is loving your body. Accepting it as it is and using it. Sensuality is the first and maybe the most important key. Because sensuality is nothing more than living with all our senses turned on. Being aware and mindful of the present. Being tuned into and turned on by what is right in front of us.

Can you live a sensuous life all day, every day? Can you be in your body, really here, feeling into this moment?

Feeling into this moment

> I see the deep green palm frond move gently in the breeze.
> I hear the wind as it rustles the fronds and the wind chimes singing.
> I taste the sweet bitterness of coffee on my tongue.
> I feel the hard, slimness of the pen in my hand.
> I catch, wafting on the breeze, the scent of nearby rain.

Chapter 2

The Journey with My Wild Feminine Spirit

> "Let the waters settle and you will see the moon and the stars mirrored in your own being." – Rumi

My journey has been ongoing for several years. I have always been a "feeling" person—perceiving most of my world through feelings and perceptions.

I wanted to embrace all my emotions, feel them fully. I often felt "wild" but most of the time just called it "weird" because it didn't fit into how I was expected to be—a good girl, quiet, not emotional, not using my own voice, not rocking the boat (or at least not out in the open). Some of those expectations were spoken, others just assumed.

Most coming from a patriarchal society and patriarchal religions. It was the culture in which many of us grew up.

Though I reached my teens during the sexual revolution, accepting that type of sexuality and living it was still not acceptable in the Bible Belt of the South. Even in my youth, I felt that there was a sacredness in sex. Those feelings of ecstasy and bliss felt divine to me.

So I kept my sexuality hidden. Few people, other than my lovers, knew my true nature, my true essence, all of me. And though I knew that real part of me, living that way in my outer world didn't always feel comfortable. Others didn't live that way. To them I was weird. But I never lost touch with my wild feminine because within, in private, I always embraced Her—my wildness, my softness, my sensuality.

Movement was the way I began expressing my wild feminine. I have always found movement to be appealing and satisfying. In my twenties I began running and weight training. I loved how movement made my body and my spirit feel alive. It was an acceptable way to embrace all the sensations in my body. Because of this, I have always loved and accepted and appreciated my body because of what it did for me. I think movement is an important key to loving our bodies.

I am a woman predominantly filled with the elements of fire and water. My fire element was very strong in my thirties and early forties, always striving, pushing, doing, over and over.

As I began to study yoga in my early forties, I found myself embracing my wild feminine even more, and beginning to live my life outwardly with her, with less fear of being weird. I learned through reading, studying, and living my wild spirit that there was another way to live, another way to be. I didn't always have to push and strive. I could let my wild feminine nature be receptive. In other words, open myself up to receiving what I desired. I could ask for what I needed and wanted. Life didn't have to be so difficult—always pushing to get what I thought I needed—or pretty much not living in the moment but rather always "when I do this" or "when I have that."

Life could be easier, more fluid, just by being present with what is and opening up my heart and body to receive it all. I learned that living with ease and presence wasn't weird at all. Maybe this wasn't how everyone lived, but it was still not weird. I began to embrace all of me, not just inwardly, but outwardly. Living my life bit by bit led by my wild feminine nature, appreciating the cycles of my emotions, the cycles of my life.

As I moved more and more into yoga, especially Tantric yoga, I felt more and more connected and in love with Mother Earth and Mama Moon. Both taught me to appreciate and live through and with cycles—cycles of doing and being, of busyness and rest, of light and darkness, of ecstasy and despair. From them I learned that all my emotions are powerful and necessary. Through them I could create magic.

This was a journey of many years and not something that happened overnight. I took one step at a time. But what a sweet journey it has been and still is. Yours will be the same way.

And along the way, you will pick and choose what resonates with you and your wild holy nature. That is the sweetness and even holiness of our wild feminine. We are all unique. Our paths are different yet we are all embracing our divine feminine.

And when we do, collectively we are amazingly powerful, using our bodies and our emotions, our wildness, to gift us with rich, sensual lives, to right injustices for all people, to protect Mother Earth and all her creatures. We feel one with all, one with everything, embracing it all and shying away from no part of our shadows. We are strong and compassionate and powerful.

We know that we don't need to be "fixed." We're not "weird." We are wild, holy, fierce, and feminine. We are her.

A few years ago, my life, as I knew it at the time, began to fall apart. Slowly at first, and then it began disintegrating quickly. For twenty-five years I had lived with and then was married to my soul mate, a happy, passionate, long-term love affair for us both. He was a sensitive, intelligent soul. One whom the sorrows of life touched too deeply. To escape his demons, he turned to alcohol.

I still don't know what his demons were, but he was never able to escape them, no matter how hard either of us tried. I thought in the beginning that my love for him was so great that my love alone would save him. I wouldn't give up. I couldn't bring myself to admit that he alone could save himself, until that truth stared me down time and time again and I had to admit defeat. I couldn't fight his demons.

I have never been in such despair. I was brought to my knees over and over again. Family and close friends did their best to just hold me up. Their love and faith in my strength helped me hold on when I felt like I could no longer. I wanted to just loosen my grip and slip away into the despair of nothingness. That would be better than where I was.

My belief in my wild feminine self, the magic that is within me, and the practices and rituals I had been practicing for several years gave me the strength I needed. I knew I was one with the Earth and all her elements. I knew the wisdom and strength of the goddess, my wild feminine, would pull me through the darkness. Just having these practices gave me strength daily.

And just like my journey practice had been, I took it just one baby step at a time. But deep inside, my belief was strong. Often I had to really dig for it. Other times, to my surprise, it would bubble to the surface. For all of it, I was grateful.

In connecting with the strength inside me, I was also able to live in that place of not-knowing, and within that not-knowing, being able to trust that I would be okay, that life had my back.

Being able to be present and live in that not-knowing is a basic part of living within our wild holy selves. Our culture, and our minds, always want to know the answers, the outcome, of everything. The wild feminine way is knowing that not-knowing is true and honest and, most of all, real.

We fool ourselves when we think we know the answers. Accepting and being in the place of not knowing anything about where my life was going saved me. And now I have learned that the place of not-knowing actually has its own sweetness.

Within the last year I lost my husband—my best friend and soul mate, I lost my daddy, and I lost my sweet kitty, Abraham. My practices and living from my wild, holy self gave me solace. I am making it through, day by day, step by step. And I feel that life is good, that life is magical.

What I have been through, just like all you have been through, are just expressions of our humanness, and the feelings of pain, despair, joy, and sweetness are so beautiful to me. I am alive.

I am real. I feel it all.

And living within and from our feminine power, we embrace it all. And this embracing makes it easier to heal.

My desire is to live from my wild feminine, to surrender and be driven by my true wild nature, that part of me (and all women) that has been with me since the beginning of time, that feminine fire that was breathed into me with the first breath I took. I want to live with that fire, that passion, that wild source of true feeling, dipping into the juicy ripe core of everything that is me, that is woman. All of it. And I can't live that way without feeling deeply, without immersing myself in all of life—sorrows as well as passion, embracing my demons as well as spirit guides. I want to feel it all. I want to live with openness, to moan, scream, cry, laugh, touch, bite, fuck, love. My wild feminine self is all of these things. And, oh so often, sex has been my best teacher.

Using our bodies for meditation

These next two meditations will bring you into the feelings and sensations of your body.

A gentle moving meditation

Sometimes our feminine bodies desire to move in meditation rather than just sit. So let's explore your body. Sit with me for a few moments. Find a quiet space. Maybe sit on a cushion or a chair if you're more comfortable. Notice how it feels to just sit. Feel the stillness begin to settle around you. Feel your breath as it moves in and out of your body. Staying close to the feeling of your breath, begin to gently move your upper body in a circular motion over your hips and pelvis, very slowly, just noticing any sensations in your body as you move. Let this movement feel organic—however it looks is perfect.

As you continue to move your upper body very fluidly, deepen your breath. Close your eyes. Feel your movements rather than thinking them. You will feel yourself gently gliding over your hips and pelvis. If your body wishes, let it take over. See where your body wants to take you.

Can you feel your spine softening a little, your belly letting go just a little? What happens when you feel softness and fluidity in your body? Can you let go a little more? And if your mind starts to kick in and question, just let it know that everything is okay and come back to the sensation of your breath and your gently moving body.

Continue to relax into this feeling. As you slow down even more, begin to make your circles smaller and smaller, until eventually you stop. Keep your eyes closed. Place your hands on your belly, palms down below your belly button. Gently feel your belly. Place your awareness there. What do you sense? What do you hear? Listen, breathe, and wait. This is your essence, the center of your being. Connect with her. If you feel the need to continue slowly moving your body, do so. Listen as you move. Touch, feel.

After a few minutes, pause and take a few deep breaths. Slowly open your eyes. If you wish, journal about your feelings, sensations.

This is a beautiful easy meditation to come back to often, allowing yourself just to check in and drop into your body.

We live in a culture that encourages us to be constantly doing. Though you may not be used to it, it is okay to stop, to pause, to just be. It's okay to slow down. In fact, you must do so if you want to awaken your wildness, your wild softness. When we slow down, we see and hear things that we miss when we're flying and running from one to-do to another. Your wildness is there, waiting for you to let her out. She wants to love fiercely, to be free, to run wild, to touch deeply and be touched.

Slow down and talk with her. Listen deeply. She will speak to you with emotions. Your wild softness brings abundance to your life. She is courageous, willing to open her heart and receive life as fully as possible, to feel it all because it is so beautiful to feel.

Our bodies, our spirits are made for feeling. How much have you felt lately? Have you opened yourself up—your heart and your body—to feel unabashedly, unapologetically, to laugh, cry, bleed, moan with ecstasy, drop to your knees in surrender? Have you felt all your emotions?

We can't just choose to open up to certain emotions. If we close ourselves off to pain, we also close ourselves off from pleasure. We must experience them all. In the end, we are grateful for them all because we realize our humanness. To be human is to be burst open to feel it all. To embrace it all.

One of my favorite poets, Mary Oliver, says, "I tell you this to break your heart, by which I mean only that it break open and never close again to the rest of the world."

When our hearts break open, we know we are alive. We feel it in our bones, our marrow. We feel rich, juicy, full. We can hold so many emotions, many of them contradictory.

That's what being human is all about—those sweet contradictory feelings.

Poet Mark Nepo calls it "the sweet ache of being human." There is nothing more amazing. Truly.

A meditation for listening to the whispers in our flesh and trusting them

When we drop into our bodies we find an immense wisdom there, an ancient wisdom that is all-knowing. We may have forgotten it, but it is always waiting for us.

Close your eyes. Breathe a deep breath in and out slowly. Feel your breath as it moves into your body. With eyes closed, begin to gently sway your body again, moving to your own body's natural rhythms. Let your body guide you. No worries; there is no right or wrong way to move. Just follow your breath.

Drop even deeper into your body. Feel the movement in your belly, your pelvis. As you sway, place your hands on your belly, fingers spread, skin touching skin, if possible. Listen. Listen deeply. What do you hear? Can you feel your aliveness, your wholeness? Continue with soft, flowing movements for as long as it feels right, gently brushing your fingers over your skin.

As you breathe deeply, sigh your exhales, long, deep. Moan if it feels good. Trust yourself, trust your body.

We get to know ourselves through our bodies. Our beautiful bodies hold our true essence, that deep feminine part of us. As you explore your body and drop inside, you will begin to find yourself, the real, authentic you. The you that can't be put into a box, that can't be stifled by rules, by shoulds and have-tos. Find her. Take as long as you need, because she is so worth it. And the journey inward is a beautiful one—often sad, disturbing, confusing—but always healing. Who are you really? Step inside yourself and discover and uncover. Magic awaits. Pure magic.

When our Shakti energy is high we experience pleasure in all aspects of our lives. Our creative energy creates our lives. Without it, we are bored and feel there is no meaning to life, no excitement. But when we are filled with sexual energy, we have the desire and the fire to create whatever we want. We feel magical and we see life as magical.

We create our own abundance. When we truly own our sexual energy, we find, or create, pleasure from everything. We enjoy pleasure. Finding pleasure in life encourages us to find even more pleasure, pleasure in the mundane places of life—simple pleasures.

Sexual energy is so much more than just sex. Even if we are alone and have no partner, maybe aren't even interested in having a partner, we still need and desire that sexual energy, our Shakti. Simply because sexual energy makes life magical. It gives us pleasure and happiness in everything.

That's how important it is. We cannot embrace our feminine energy, our wild feminine, without owning and honoring our sexuality.

How is your sexual energy? Is it vibrant, or have you let it simply dry up? Do you tell yourself it's not important anyway, knowing that is not how you feel deep inside? Do you feel alive and juicy, like a sexy woman? Or are you shamed by your sexual feelings, or maybe feel as if you don't deserve to be sexual?

Just being honest with yourself is the first step. It is perfectly okay to feel any or all of the above. Be gentle with yourself, and from this gentleness let's see if we can shake up your Shakti, even just a little. Are you ready to try? I promise your life will change. Remember, you're never too old or too busy to become re-acquainted with your wild, sexy self, whether you ever use it for sex or not. But I hope you do.

So where do we start? Shakti starts with you—no one else—and certainly not a sexual partner. You will begin to feel your wild woman wake up, coming alive, as you begin to explore your pleasures. And remember, feeling sexy or sexual looks different on every woman. Be yourself, your sexy self. Oh, this is such a fun journey.

And if you say, "Okay, but I am already full of and thoroughly enjoying my sexual energy," I am so happy. And I promise you that this exploration will bring even more sensual pleasures into your life. Your wild woman wants to kick it up a notch. Are you ready to give that a try?

So where do we begin? We begin with ourselves and our bodies, our senses. After all, that's what sensual pleasures are—just the pleasure of all our senses. Learning to "feel" our sensations, our pleasures. This is getting out of our heads and into our bodies.

In truth, embracing our wildness is about feeling rather than thinking. Moving out of our heads and into our bellies and hearts and living from those places. It is being present. As a wild and holy woman, it is our spiritual path. And it feels luscious.

We awaken our wild feminine by opening our hearts, moving our bodies, loving our bodies, feeling all our emotions, creating ritual, opening to receive, and by embracing our sensuality and sexuality. All of these bring us into the present moment. All are moments of mindfulness.

Opening your heart

One of the keys to embracing your wildness is to open your heart. To live a life of juicy richness we must open our hearts and be vulnerable. And it is scary to open ourselves, knowing that at some point we will be hurt. But we are not really living, we are not experiencing our humanness unless we feel both joy and pain. In order to feel the love, we must experience the sorrow.

This brings us to our wildness, our divine feminine. If we've never been brought to our knees, we will never experience the pure heights of ecstasy and passion, because our hearts are locked away. We are afraid to open and really, really love. Maybe we've been hurt before and don't want to be hurt again. It was just too painful. But until we open our hearts fully and allow ourselves to love passionately and freely, our lives will be dull, unimaginative, grey. When we make the decision to open our hearts, to be raw and real, our lives become vibrant hues. Your life is a canvas. What colors are you painting today? Are you using big brush strokes or whisper-thin lines? Which will make you happier?

When we begin to embrace our wildness, she shows us how to open and trust. Not just love, but to trust life and the universe. We begin to understand that it is a necessity. We cannot be wild and holy and fierce and be afraid to love. We cannot be afraid to touch life and be touched by life. To make love to life and let life make love to us.

Journaling prompts for you

Journaling prompts are simply questions for you to ponder and write about. Just write the question and begin to answer without censoring yourself. Remember these writings are just for your eyes. Be honest with yourself.

- ✶ How am I touching life right now?
- ✶ How can I honor the soft animal of my body?
- ✶ How can I practice being mindful about pleasure?

Treating our soft animal bodies as the sacred vessels they are brings our wildness to the surface from its buried depths. Not mindless pleasures, but mindful pleasures, those pleasures that nourish and support us, that make us feel alive, not numb. What are those pleasures for you? What stirs you up, makes your heart sing and your face smile?

To embrace our wild feminine and open our hearts, we must journey inward. Oh, how much we learn from ourselves when we do that. Often it's not easy and sometimes it's just plain difficult, but oh so worth it as we begin to really feel ourselves.

One of the best things I've found from moving out of my head and into my heart is the beautiful, awe-inspiring feeling of presence. Being right here, in this moment, and, no matter what is actually happening, just being present in my body and in my senses is somehow always peaceful, underneath the chaos. Kind of like a tumultuous, roaring ocean. Yet if you drop below the surface, you find stillness. Being present amidst the chaos of humanness is like that.

I've found the best way to bring myself to this moment quickly is to drop into my body because our bodies are always in this moment, no matter what else is going on. When we are present, we are only dealing with what is happening now, not what we fear might happen or our worries of what has already happened. Both scenarios are in our heads.

So just using my breath to drop into my body and journey inward is a quick way to feel alive, to let go of anxiety and just be, to just appreciate what I feel at this very moment—my breath, my heartbeat, my feeling of touch. These all bring me home. Home to myself, home to this moment. And in this moment, I can usually find some pleasure, and then pleasure itself brings me into my body.

I cannot experience pleasure and not be in this moment. That's why pleasure is so important to our being, our wild softness. Our feminine wildness desires pleasure—meaningful, sweet pleasure. Those pleasures that accentuate this moment. Not numbing pleasures that take us away from life. There's a big difference.

On our inward journey, as we open our hearts, we discover what brings us real pleasure and joy.

> "I do take advantage of, you know, feeling sensual and feeling sexy. And I think that is tremendously empowering . . . . I feel that any woman who is in touch with her femininity and sensuality is a woman that is empowered." – Shakira

> "I disregard the proportions, the measures, the tempo of the ordinary world. I refuse to live in the ordinary world as ordinary women, to enter ordinary relationships. I want ecstasy." – Anais Nin

Chapter 3

Who Are You?

"Surrender to the deluge. Know it as
your own. This ocean of bliss is you."
− Radiance Sutras, Tantra Text

Who are you? Really, who are you, right here, right now? Who are you without all your titles, your roles, your names, your skills? Who are you? Deep down inside . . . the true essence of you . . . your true nature.

Maybe you've asked yourself this question many times, or maybe you've been afraid to ask that question. It can be a very uncomfortable, sometimes frustrating, question. But asking the question is so important. Who are we without other's opinions, voices, judgments? Who are we when we just grow still and quiet and ask ourselves that question?

Do you feel as if you are greatly influenced by others? If so, when and how? The answer to that question "who are you?" will sometimes change as you grow and change yourself. And yet some parts will stay the same. What is uniquely you? Do you love what is uniquely you? That is what loving yourself is all about.

Do you ever feel you try to change yourself in any way in order to fit in? When do you see this most often? Does it involve your looks or your behaviors? Or both? Do you feel you have to look or act a certain way for one of the roles you play? Or are you now more comfortable with who you truly are? Do you know who you are, and can you also be and act and look as you truly are?

When we are so grounded and centered into who we are, who we truly are, then it's easy to not care what others think or want. Not a flippant kind of "I don't care," but rather a deep understanding and feeling of who we are . . . who we really are. And we don't need others to see us in a certain way.

Use your own language to know yourself, to describe yourself. Not others' words. Not words you think you should be. To decide what truly works for each of us, we have to ask the question and begin to know who we really are. Sometimes just changing our language changes how we feel. Through changing our language we honor ourselves.

Meditation—who am I?

Find a quiet spot to sit. Take several deep full breaths, relaxing your body. Take your time moving into your body, just noticing how you feel. Once you have allowed yourself to breathe and relax, take your awareness to your heart space. Placing your hands on your heart, breathe into your heart. Take a moment to be grateful and feel your heart space opening and expanding with love.

When you feel ready, ask yourself, "Who am I in my deepest part? Who am I?" Just notice what feelings arise. Whatever first comes up is okay and perfect. Keep asking the question for a few moments, listening for sensations as well as words. If you hear words, how do those words resonate in your body?

After a few moments, ask yourself, "What does my heart/body want or need?" Again, sit with the question and just notice. Just feel. When you feel ready, take a long, sighing exhale and open your eyes. Move your body gently.

And if it feels right, take your journal and answer the next few questions. Try to free-write—just whatever pops into your mind first—without censoring, just letting your hand keep moving over the page.

These journaling prompts are excellent to use as often as you'd like. Usually, each time, you're able to go a little deeper.

* What do I love?
* What excites me, body and soul?
* What things am I most passionate about?
* When not immersed in my roles, who am I?
* What do very few people know about me?
* If I had all the time in the world, what would I do? How would I spend my time?
* What do I wish I could say?
* What three words describe me best?
* Use this phrase as a writing prompt: If you really knew me, you'd know _____.

There is a place in all of us that is filled with creativity, flows with spontaneity and curiosity, and trusts the not-knowing. Magic is within us. This is who we really are—our true essence. Connecting deeply with our breath and our bodies takes us to who we really are. Invite yourself there now. Take the time to know who you really are in all your messiness and beauty. Come back to this place again and again.

A nourishing meditation

When we take the time to nourish our spirits, we begin to see our true selves. We get in touch with our authenticity. How do you nourish yourself? Do you enjoy giving your body and your spirit nourishment and love? Or is nourishing yourself something you neglect, giving all of you to others? You can only continue to give to others if you nourish your own body, mind, and spirit regularly.

Let's settle in for a little meditation to help you begin to listen to and know what you need to nourish yourself right now. Get to know yourself a little bit better.

So take a comfortable seat. Maybe that's lying down. Take a moment to feel the earth underneath you and settle into her. When you're ready, take a deep breath in, all the way into your belly, and then softly sigh it out through your mouth.

Let the soft rhythmic flow of your breath begin to soften your body. Take your time. No hurry. Just feel the gentle flow of your breath, like water, moving through your body. As it flows through you, touching every part of you, you feel your muscles and skin growing soft and relaxed. Invite yourself deeper into that feeling. Yes, that's it. Go a little deeper into your body. Enjoy the softening, the release.

Maybe a little smile is coming to your lips—just a soft one, a little smile of joy and contentment because you've been here before. You remember how sweet this feels, these moments when you are present with your own body and breath. Sink in a little deeper. Just let yourself be breathed. You are just the vessel.

As you read these questions, just let them wash over you. Don't search for answers in your mind. Just feel the words. Let them move over you and into you with your breath. Notice how your body feels and responds as you hear the questions.

- How would I feel if I were completely nourished?
- What does my body need to feel completely nourished?
- What nourishes my spirit?
- How might I respond to life differently if I were completely nourished?

Just let yourself be with the questions. How do these questions feel in your body? Just notice, just feel, just breathe. If you were completely nourished, from the inside, who would you be? What actions might you take? Continue to let your breath flow through you.

When you feel ready, bring your hands to your heart, placing your palms on your skin if you can. Say to your heart, "What do you need, dear one, to feel completely nourished?" Listen and feel. Now bring your hands to your belly, palms on skin, and ask, "What do you need, dear one, to feel completely nourished?" Just breathe.

When you are ready, close your meditation by thanking your body, your breath, and your spirit. Have a moment of deep gratitude for all you are.

Then slowly open your eyes and gently move your body.

I invite you now to journal about your feelings as you asked yourself these questions, just writing down whatever thoughts and emotions came to you as you meditated. See what shows up as you freely write.

Come back to these questions often, giving yourself the time to see what you need to feel completely nourished in body, mind, and spirit. Namaste.

This life of ours is a mystery. None of us knows what our lives will bring or who will come into our lives and who will leave us. Life is an unknown, but I do know that when I begin to trust, when I know who I am, when I begin to live in that "not-knowing" without fear, my life is sweet. When I can accept the not-knowing and look at it expectantly as a mystery—a good mystery—then my life flows. Rather than having anxiety about the unknown, I believe and trust that much of that mystery will be good—maybe even exciting. And it truly works.

I also know that living authentically, living from my heart, just feels right. It makes the mystery of life seem a little less mysterious. And when I let my deepest inner self, my body and heart, lead the way, I begin to trust the unknown, to be comfortable living in that space of not-knowing.

And I have found the best way to live from my truest wild self is to spend quiet time with myself, just breathing, dropping into my body and asking myself, "What do I need right now?" "Who am I right this moment?" Doing this regularly keeps me centered and grounded and when I am centered and grounded I am more likely to know my heart's desire.

Guided imagery meditation—your free spirit

Begin to settle in. I like to do many of my meditation practices or embodiment practices lying down. So feel free to snuggle into your bed or just rest on your mat. Take a deep breath in through your nose and let out a long sigh through your mouth. Let your sigh be as loud or as soft as feels good to you. Do this a few more times until you begin to feel your entire body softening. Then begin to just soften and deepen your breath. Feel it as it moves through you. Welcome it in. Relax a little more.

Now let's use our imagination. Let's take a walk on the beach. As you walk by the water, feel the sand between your toes. It's cool to your feet because the sun is just coming up. You feel a soft breeze on your face. You can almost taste the salty air. As you walk, breathing softly, you begin to feel so calm and then you notice that feelings of love and joy, even passion and freedom, are moving softly through your body. You feel a passion, a desire, for this life that is yours.

You notice how it feels to pay attention to that part of you that feels free, that doesn't have to fit into someone's ideal, that part of you that is vibrant and alive and knows that perfection is not important.

Maybe you remember a time when life just felt right because you felt free to express yourself in your own way. You were trusting your own guidance. There was an inner spark, a magic that is YOU.

So in this moment, tap into that place again. Feel your spark, your magic, that belief in yourself. Trust it. Trust yourself. Revel in this feeling. Let this feeling, this spark, sink into your body.

After a few more moments of savoring this magical feeling, bring your awareness back to the ocean waves lapping at your toes. As you gaze at the horizon, know it is time to leave the beach. Before you leave, promise yourself that you will keep this spark, this magic. Hold this feeling in your body as you turn to leave.

The wild feminine self holds all of our emotions. We are constantly changing, just like the moon, the ocean. We are nature itself made of earth, water, air, and fire. We will not always be positive, or eager, or happy. We are a container for all our emotions, and our wild self wants to feel them all. We embrace our changing moods, knowing it is part of our humanness—our wildness. And through it all, we know who we are. We know we are all of these. We know that who we are is contradiction and we learn to embrace the mystery that is us.

And so we ask ourselves, how can we use our sadness, our anger, our joy, our passion to fully live our lives, to move forward, to create change, for ourselves and others?

Chapter 4

Presence

"The aim of life is to live, and to live means to be aware, joyously, drunkenly, serenely, divinely aware." – Henry Miller

Our wild feminine Shakti energy is a way to bring us into the present moment. When we are immersed in our Shakti energy, we are right here, right now. There is nothing else. And embracing and living within our wild feminine self is a beautiful way to be fully present. Because our wild feminine desires this moment, she doesn't waste her time with regrets or wishing forward. She knows that this present moment is the most powerful and that's where she lives. Because she is filled with passion, desire, compassion, and love, the present moment is where she thrives. So as you begin to embrace your wild self more and more you will find that you want to be in this moment. You notice that it is not nearly as peaceful or passionate in the past or the future. You and everyone else in your life thrive when you are in the present moment.

Our feminine energy is vitally connected to our senses—all of them. You may have noticed that presence is all about being fully embodied or, in other words, being fully in your body. The quickest way to drop down into your body is to use your senses, slowing down and noticing what you see right before you. What sounds and smells do you notice? These quickly draw you into your body and will anchor you there. What are you touching, or what is touching you?

You may say, well, I'm always using my senses. And, yes, you are correct. But much of the time we are not intimately aware of them. We see without really noticing, we eat without really tasting, we touch without really feeling. Senses are being used, but we are not feeling them. What a difference in our lives and in our relationships when we really start to connect with our senses. We see and feel things we have never felt before. And it is so sweet and pleasurable—sometimes bittersweet, yes—but oh so worth it.

Our breath is another sense we use to anchor ourselves into the present moment. Really just feeling ourselves breathe, noticing it, and maybe then beginning to deepen and lengthen the breath. As we draw our breath deep into our bodies, we begin to calm our nervous systems. This allows us to feel more, to see more. As we move into our bodies with our breath, we begin to notice how our bodies are feeling. We may notice tension and tightness that, up until this point, we didn't know we had.

And when we are aware of and living through our senses, we are present. Our senses are actually a very easy way to navigate our way back into this moment because, let's face it, most of us yearn to really be fully alive in this moment. Yet we are so often pulled out of the present by our past, usually things we wish we'd done, or drawn into the future by wanting something other than what is right in front of us.

How much of your life do you think you have missed by being in either the past or the future? And when we are not in the present moment, we miss all the magical mysteries that unfold in front of us daily. We just don't even notice them. Just think of all the magic you may have missed along the way.

Though living and being in the present sounds easy and simple, it is often difficult to accomplish. Especially in the beginning. But we can teach ourselves to be present. It is a practice. Like anything else, with practice we get much better at it. And one of the things that keeps pulling us back to the present is because it just feels so fucking good. The more time we spend there, the more we notice how beautiful and serene our lives can be, even amidst chaos and confusion. We have more clarity in the present moment.

There are three places we can find ourselves—the past where our lives have already happened, the future where we are wishing or worrying about what will happen, and this very moment that is happening right before us. Sadly, it is the very moment that is happening right in front of us that is the most difficult for most of us to remain in. We tend to be either fixated on the past, filled with regrets and guilt or desire to have it again, or we are dreaming (or often worrying) about the future, saying things such as, "When I get a new job I will be happy" or "When my children grow up I will have the time to write my book." Always looking forward or back. The problem with this is that we miss our "real" lives because our real lives are happening at this very moment. Life can only be lived in the present, otherwise you are missing it.

So how does this present moment look? Often we feel or believe that our lives, our moments, are so mundane. And yet that is where the magic lives. The most ordinary moments are the present moments that truly are "our lives." Those ordinary moments are where we live, and when we are truly "there" for them they are not ordinary at all. They are extremely special.

If you are not present, you will miss that magical moment of your child excitedly telling you about the redbird he saw. Or you will miss that moment of looking into your lover's eyes—really looking. Or how about that moment when you are holding a hot, steaming cup of coffee in your hands and you pause to take a deep breath. Be there for any of these and your life begins to slow down and the pleasure seeps back in. You feel an ease in your body and maybe even a smile coming to your face. Because you notice. You are here.

And the same is true for even those difficult moments in life. By just being present with them, accepting them just as they are in that moment without wanting them to be different (which is not being present), we can begin to feel a little ease within the pain or challenge. We will find ourselves feeling peaceful even with the trouble. Because we are just present with it. And from this place we always find that we have more clarity and can make decisions from a place of responding rather than reacting.

I have many ways I remind myself to be present. One is with words. I am a big believer in affirmations and the power of words—both written and spoken. You may have heard me say before, "Our words are magic spells. They are manifestations themselves."

I write words on everything in my home—my tile floors, chalkboard walls, mirrors, tables. And many of the words I write are to remind me to live in this moment: Just be here right now, Live this moment, This moment is all that matters, What turns you on today?, and even a humorous Where are you now? So that as I move through my house I am reminded to be here now, to be present with whatever is happening. And often these reminders just make me smile. What could be better that that, right? I invite you to try it. Just gentle reminders throughout your surroundings. Maybe a message or screen saver on your phone or computer. Just a reminder to come back to sensing and feeling, to get out of your head and into your body.

Our wild feminine doesn't live in our heads. She's much too free-spirited for that. She is wild and free and full of feelings, all one feels. And as she feels, she is present, always living in the now, not in some pretend "when this happens." She's also not one for guilt and living in the past.

The more you live from your wildness, the more in the moment you will be. And you'll begin to truly desire those "in the moment" times because they are so rich. And they are so rich because you are feeling, touching, seeing, tasting. You are here.

When we are living in the present moment, we are fully embodied. This fact actually makes returning (and hopefully remaining) in the present moment pretty easy. By bringing ourselves to our senses, even just one of them, we will drop ourselves back into this moment. By just noticing the smells or looking closely at what is right in front of you, you drop into your body and at the same time you drop into the present moment. Then you begin to slowly bring up your other senses, using them all to anchor yourself in the moment. This can be done at any time or any place and just takes a moment. But awareness is the key. You must begin to quickly notice when you are away from your body and stuck in your head—maybe ruminating or worrying. Because only then can you bring yourself back to this moment. This beautiful, precious moment. So in reality, all you need is a desire to be fully in your body all the time. Fully embodied. In this way, you will be in this moment—always.

That's what embracing your wild feminine divine nature is all about. Being in our bodies. And being in our bodies will certainly change our lives for the better. Bringing about much richness and fullness and abundance, greater joy and pleasure, pure orgasmic pleasure for life. Sounds amazing, doesn't it? It can be yours and it can be mine. Just by being present.

For a few moments let's examine how presence looks in our lives. As always, feel free to substitute things that resonate with you.

Being present is standing with your two feet bare on the earth, feeling the ground beneath you. Sand between your toes. It is feeling a breeze on your face. It is noticing how blue the sky really is. Presence is seeing the cardinal moving through the bamboo as you sip your coffee. Being present is sometimes feeling that you are mired in mud—feeling stuck and just being with it. Presence is feeling tears well up in your eyes and overflowing onto your cheeks, without stopping them.

Sometimes presence is hearing a loved one saying difficult words you may not want to hear, but looking them in the eyes and fully listening. Presence is living from your heart, which sometimes cracks open. Presence is also feeling a warm smile in your body and noticing when someone smiles at you.

Presence is being aware in your body that each and every moment is sacred and powerful and, most of all, a gift. Presence does not take these moments for granted, even, and maybe especially, if they are difficult and challenging. Each is a gift.

Presence is full of gratitude for it all. Gratitude is a most meaningful way to be present.

Presence doesn't require thinking or planning ahead. Presence is noticing what is right in front of you right this moment.

Presence is a blessing, an affirmation, an "I love you and appreciate you" to each and every moment of our lives. Presence is knowing how precious life is, and how fleeting.

Being present is standing in the rain, feeling each and every drop of rain touch your skin. Present is noticing a rainbow as you sit at a traffic light. Present is stopping to take three deep full breaths into your belly as you look at the world around you. Being present is taking it all in. Presence is listening to your lover, not with your mind, but with your body.

Presence is touching your own skin purposefully and enjoying the sensations. Being present is holding space for, and maybe holding in your arms, a suffering friend, with no thoughts of fixing or changing, rather just being there for them in this present moment. Presence is being able to hold your suffering self in this same place, gently being with what is.

When we allow ourselves to be with what is—surrendering to the moment—we find a kind of peace. A gentleness. A sweetness. And from that place we can eventually make better decisions. That clarity requires presence.

What does presence mean to you? How do you feel when you are present with everything that is happening? Being present is the way most of us want to live our lives. Because we know that when we are present everything and everyone looks brighter, fuller, almost magical. And being present sounds like it would be so simple, right? Simple it is, but easy, not necessarily. Being present requires awareness on our part so that we know quickly when we have moved out of being present and into the past or the future.

Some journaling prompts for you:

* What does presence or being present feel like to me?
* How does being present show up in my body?
* What beautiful, magical moments have I had while being present?
* What things bring me back into the present moment when I realize I've wandered away? Make a list.
* Why do I desire to be present?

Presence has nothing to do with perfect. Often we don't want to be present because our "present" isn't as perfect as we wish or as perfect as we think another's present is. Presence is never perfect. There is no such thing as perfect. There is just the raw, beautiful, messy, breathtaking, and heartbreaking joy of being human. That is presence. And there is nothing better.

Presence, or being present, is being rooted fully into reality. Not pessimism but the reality of this very moment, of what is happening right now before our very eyes and in our very-much present body. Standing in that reality without denying it or wishing painfully for it to be different. Either of these two actions is mind-oriented and will make us unhappy.

When you are truly present with what is happening, there is a calm presence underneath it all. Presence is knowing and believing that everything is sacred. No matter how plain or mundane, there is great sacredness in that plainness.

Presence is knowing that we are sacred, our bodies are sacred. Presence is trusting that the universe, or goddess, or your idea of divinity, has your back. That you are a co-creator of your life, but you are not in control. Presence teaches us to be comfortable with not-knowing, or the unknown, and that is a valuable lesson.

When we become comfortable living in the unknown or not-knowing, life just seems easier. It seems more magical and mysterious. Albert Einstein said, "There are only two ways to live your life: as though nothing is a miracle, or as though everything is a miracle." The present moment is miraculous and mysterious and sweet in all its mystery.

As we find ourselves pausing more often, bringing ourselves back into our bodies and being "here," we begin to feel the difference in our lives. Only when we are present can we feel the richness of truly being human and experience all the sensations and feelings that make us feel alive and raw and real. Nothing is better. This is what we are meant for. And when we feel, when we are alive in our bodies, we see the magic all around us, we see the abundance all around us, and we want to be there all the time. It feels so deliciously sweet that we desire to come back to this place, this realness, this presence, this rawness that is who we are and where we live. It is our wild feminine self in all its glory. When we visit this present place often enough, we begin to crave living there. We find peace and fullness there. And from this place of presence we can so much more easily care for our loved ones, having more of ourselves to give. And this, in turn, makes our lives richer and fuller and sweeter. Not always happy but deeper and more meaningful.

And it only requires giving this moment—and whoever or whatever we are doing in this moment—our full, unwavering attention. One of my favorite quotes from Henry Miller says, "The moment one gives close attention to anything, even a blade of grass, it becomes a mysterious, awesome, indescribably magnificent world itself." How true that is. And that is why when we are giving all our moments our full presence we begin to feel the extraordinary just beneath the ordinary. Our lives are full of extraordinary moments that are just waiting and hoping to be discovered. The ordinary is no longer ordinary—it is extraordinary. It is much like looking at life through the eyes of a child. That wonder about everything—often because it is being seen for the very first time—sometimes over and over again! Children have a delightful way of seeing the mundane. This is what we are embracing when we live in the present moment. This beautiful feeling of wonder, of amazement.

How might you begin to look at everything in a different light? It is amazing how things change as we begin to look at them with fresh eyes. A fresh perspective gives new life to everything and everyone. What if you began to look at your lover or partner as if you knew nothing about them? No preconceived notions of how they think or how they will respond. Our communications would be so different. This is what happens when we begin to live in the moment. All sorts of things change and open up. Because we are looking at life, at our lives, with brand new eyes—a new awareness.

Living like this also brings forth so much gratitude. We begin to see how much we truly have rather than thinking I wish I had that or she has more than I do. Our appreciation for ourselves, for others, for so many things, begins to grow and grow. And like a beautiful circle, this makes us even more grateful.

A practice for each day—wonder

Set an intention before you get out of bed in the morning to see everything around you with new eyes, as if you had never encountered it before. Start while lying in your bed by looking around your room. Pick one or two objects that you have seen many times. Spend a few minutes REALLY looking at them as if you'd never seen them before. Look at their shape, their color, the space they inhabit, and take a moment to describe them to yourself. Then take another moment to remember why you have these objects, what they mean to you. (Because I hope your home is filled with only those things that you love and that spark feeling for you.)

Now as you get out of bed, continue this journey throughout your day—seeing everything with fresh new eyes. Use all your senses. Most of all, use your sense of wonder. Use this sense of newness, of wonder, with your loved ones. Use this sense of newness with strangers you meet. Know that as you move through your day in this wonder, you will find magic—in those you love, in strangers, and even in difficult circumstances. Open yourself up to not only seeing with fresh eyes but coming from that fresh perspective making fresh new choices and decisions. See how your day unfolds. And if you find, as you move through your day, that you forget your intention, don't worry. It happens to us all. Just bring yourself back—back to the present and back to this sense of wonder. Most of us find that just living in the present moment brings a sense of wonder all on its own.

At the end of your day, reflect upon how your little experiment worked out. Try to reflect upon this with your body and senses rather than just your mind. How did you feel as you moved through your day? What was sparked? Was it easy or difficult or somewhere in between? Maybe, if you have time, journal about your responses. And maybe mention how others responded to you as you looked at them with fresh eyes and no expectations of "knowing how they always are." And, maybe, if you really enjoyed this—which I hope you did—you'll decide that you'd like to make it a daily practice. This is another way to invite yourself into the present moment again and again. Living in that sense of wonder and amazement. Your wild feminine self will be delighted.

Now you've finished your reflection upon your day. Feel a little smile on your face. Take a full deep breath into your belly and softly let it out through your mouth. Another deep breath in and a long sigh out. Take a moment to thank yourself for experimenting today and thank your body and your wild self for making your journey possible and easy. Feel softness in your body and in your mind. And now settle in to the rest of your evening or maybe settle into your cozy bed.

A deeper embodied meditation

Join me for a few moments. We're going to take a pause and settle into some stillness and quiet for a little while. Take a seat on the floor or your cushion. Maybe you want to take a few gentle stretches before we begin. How do you feel? Reach your arms overhead and slowly wave side to side. Now drop your arms to your sides and roll your shoulders back a couple of times. Feel your hips and thighs settling into the earth beneath you. Let's take a few deep breaths together. Breathe in deeply, hold for just a moment and then open your mouth and let your breath fall out, long and slow and soft. Yes, doesn't that feel sweet? Now let's do that again. Every time you sigh out your exhale, notice that your body softens just a little bit more.

If you've not already done so, gently close your eyes. Let your breath find its own rhythm. Don't rush it. There is no hurry at all. This is where you are meant to be right now. Let your breath touch your heart and heart space. Let your breath touch your belly. Notice the crown of your head . . . notice the tip of your nose . . . notice the palms of your hands and maybe wiggle your fingers . . . feel your toes. Invite yourself into your body. Allow your breath to take you deeper and deeper.

What physical sensations are you noticing? Are you feeling any emotions surfacing? Be gentle with yourself.

Our bodies are so, so wise. Yet how often do we rush around, running from task to task, living in our heads and not even noticing that we have bodies? Our bodies have been with us all these years. They have carried us through everything we have ever been through—ecstatic pleasures and deep sorrows. Our bodies have always been there for us. And our bodies know things long before our minds can comprehend them. Our bodies have ancient knowledge and do their best to align us with our authenticity. When we make a decision by listening to our bodies, we know when it is authentic because we feel a sense of peace, of restfulness upon making our decision. It feels as if our bodies have just taken a deep sigh.

So let's take a moment now to just thank our bodies for being with us, even though we sometimes neglect them.

Stay close to your breath as you move even deeper into your body. Go slowly. There is no rush. Just breathe and feel. If it feels right, place your hands on your belly. Feel your breath deep into your belly and your pelvis. What does your belly want to say to you today? Just listen . . . just listen. Just breathe. What does your body want you to know today?

Now let your breath touch your heart space. Breathe. What does your heart want to say to you today? Just listen to whatever arises from your belly, your heart, your body. Be gentle with yourself with whatever you are feeling or noticing.

Listening to our bodies opens us up to vulnerability. So embrace whatever shows up with loving kindness. Trust it. Often we are afraid to listen to our bodies because we know that makes us vulnerable. But how can we truly be alive, fully live, without vulnerability? Vulnerability is what makes us human—that sweet humbling rawness of being alive. So invite it in. Open your heart. Open your belly. Feel whatever you are feeling and know that you are alive.

What does your body have to say to you today? What does your body want you to know? As you are listening, say a gentle thank you to your body. Let your body know you want it to be heard. Let your body know you love her.

One of the things I know your body will tell you every time is, "This moment is so precious. No matter how ordinary you think it might be, this moment is more precious than you can imagine." Because your body knows every precious moment that makes up your life. Your body is always present in this moment and she invites you to be there also. She desires for you to be there. Welcome yourself home.

That precious moment when you look into your lover's eyes, that moment when you hear your friend's hearty laugh, that moment when your child or grandchild excitedly tells you about her day. Let your body hold you in all these precious moments.

Slowly bring your awareness back to your breath. Once more, gently move your body, maybe moving your head side to side, wiggling fingers and toes, and putting a soft smile on your lips. Take a moment to once more thank your body for her insight and promise to talk with her again real soon. Welcome yourself home again. Slowly open your eyes and notice the room around you. See everything in its vividness, its beauty, its realness. You are home.

Chapter 5

Knowing Our Bodies as Our Home

"It is time to listen to the whispers of your body as she is tugged to dance in the light of the moon." – Molly Remer

How long has it been since you really, truly lived in your body? Felt at home there? When was the last time you felt truly, and terrifically, at home in your own skin?

To live in our wild feminine nature is to, above everything else, feel at home in our own skin. Not only to feel at home there, but to actually luxuriate there. To feel and know that your body is a sacred place—perfect just as it is—and totally yours. Do you feel that way often? To feel at home in our bodies requires that we love our bodies, truly love our bodies. Every part of them. And loving our bodies is having a comfort level with our bodies. We know, love, and trust our bodies. When we feel this way, we allow, even invite ourselves, to find pleasure in our bodies.

So many women have more of a hate relationship with their bodies than a love affair. And sometimes it is simply a neglect of our bodies and a neglect of appreciation of our bodies. When neglected for too long, it's almost as if we forget we have beautiful, feeling bodies, a uniquely sensuous place that is our home. We forget that we don't HAVE bodies, we ARE bodies.

I have worked with many clients who cannot even look at their bodies in the mirror, clothed or naked. This is so, so sad. How can your body feel that you love her if you can't even look at her?

So how do we begin that journey back into our beautiful feminine bodies? And if you're one of the lucky ones who feels at home in her skin and enjoys her body—awesome! Celebrate. And maybe expand your sensual pleasures, if you'd like. There are always new ways to enjoy and pleasure our bodies. Try something new.

Movement is one of the quickest ways to fall in love with our bodies because we begin to see our bodies in light of what they do for us, rather than how they look. In our culture, we are constantly reminded and bombarded about how our bodies "should" look. When we switch that to look at "what" our bodies allow us to do, how strong they are, how flexible, we begin to see our bodies for the amazing creatures they are.

Whether our movement is running, or yoga, or dancing, or weightlifting, we begin to notice that we find pleasure in that movement. We begin to notice that our legs enabled us to run another mile, that our bodies finally felt really sweet in a forward fold or a handstand. We begin to feel proud of our bodies. And rather than thinking that we're too fat or too thin, we begin to realize and appreciate the pleasures our bodies bring us through movement. It may take a few weeks or a few months, but our attitudes will change. Appreciation is not far from love.

I have been a runner all my life. In addition to running, I have also been a yogi and a weightlifter, all at the same time. I began moving in my early twenties and it felt so good that I never looked back. I never stopped.

Early on I began to be amazed at what my body could do when I asked it to and gave it the proper training. And you know the best part of all that movement? I fell in love with my body and I still am today—forty-something years later. I had always felt pretty good about my body, but I developed a whole new appreciation for it. I actually fell in love with how my body made me feel when I was moving—all kinds of movement.

I know movement works, and I have seen it work for so many women. But we need to approach movement not to make us look better but in order to make us feel better. And it will do just that. And when we look in the mirror, we don't see flaws, we see beautiful bodies that can run miles, or climb mountains, or just walk through nature.

We see something spectacular and amazing. We fall in love with our bodies and the pleasure they bring us. Some of those pleasures may change over time, but there are always new pleasurable ways to move our bodies.

If you've not really moved your body consistently before, begin by asking yourself what you enjoy. Do you need to be with others, as in a class setting or on a team? Or do you need alone time to balance out the rest of your day? Do you prefer to move to music, to dance? Do you need competition?

Try a few things until you hit upon something you enjoy—even if just a little. Then do it consistently. And notice, or even journal about, your feelings before, during, and after movement. You'll want to notice the tiny little changes you start to feel in your body and your spirit. Consistency is the key for developing a love of your own body. And when you finish your daily movement practice, pause to thank your body.

When I am running, I often am thanking my body—my hips, my legs, my feet—as I take every step. Our sweet bodies love to be appreciated.

And remember, your wild feminine self already loves your body. She is your body. So even if you don't feel at one with her yet, call her forth now. Let her begin to show you how to love and embrace your body. Like "acting as if." Notice how it feels. Journal about it.

How does, or would, your wild feminine self love her body? How does she show that love? Part of our self-care is looking for ways to give that soft animal body of ours what it desires. Be creative. But give your wild feminine body the care it deserves.

So let's spend a little time thinking and writing about our amazing bodies. I sometimes write a love letter to my body, especially if I am going through a rough time with her, whether physically or emotionally. I let her know all the things I cherish about her and I ask her to help me know and understand what she needs at this time.

I also sometimes just write down all the times my body has been there for me. And just writing them down brings me back to an awareness of how special she is to me. Brings me back to my wild feminine self.

I love my body. She has given me freedom as I run over streets and trails in cities near and far. Given me strength and often pleasure through many miles. I have held lovers close to my body, feeling their skin, their touch, their souls. I have cried many tears through many broken hearts. And I have also loved fiercely, smiled and laughed so often that I cannot even imagine how many smiles I have shared and felt over these years. I feel the memories of all these moments in my body. She has let me taste decadently delicious food and drink; hold babies, friends, and lovers in my arms; see wondrous sunrises and sunsets and moon rises. I move this body daily in so many ways. She lifts weights, sometimes dances and skips, she loves red wine. She sleeps and sometimes lies awake, she kisses and hugs, she reads, she writes lots!, she drinks coffee and sometimes eats donuts and coffee rolls, she loves to paint and draw, she loves intimate conversations and looking deep into the eyes of her lover. She is me and she brings me so much pleasure and she gives me the strength to make it through any suffering. She is wild and holy and fierce.

What about you? What will you write about your body? A good prompt is just "I love my body because she . . ." Begin by just free writing and see what appears. If it is a struggle, just smile softly and keep at it. If you give her a chance, your body, your wildness, will remind you of why she is so special.

Don't worry. We'll talk a lot more about being at home in our bodies and showing our bodies love when we talk about sensuality, pleasure, and sexuality.

Chapter 6

The Feminine Power of Receiving

"There is a voice that doesn't use words.
Listen." – Rumi

Receiving is a word that is often difficult for us women. Yet it is our very nature, our feminine nature, to receive. So why then is it so difficult?

We live in a masculine oriented and dominated culture. Always doing, always busy. Very independent and feeling as if we don't need help, we don't need anyone else. We can do it on our own. And yet receiving is a vital part of living well for everyone. It is nourishing and replenishing to our spirits and our bodies. And when we can ask and receive gracefully, we touch others in a very positive way. All humans want to give and all humans need to receive.

Our receiving allows others the opportunity to give. This is especially important to those who love us.

Right now I want us to just think about ourselves. Our wild feminine spirit thrives on receiving. Not just receiving from others, but receiving from the universe. From the divine, however you see it. While our masculine energy wants to be "doing," our feminine energy knows that so much can be done by just opening up to receiving. And we need a gentle balance of both. But most of us need to re-learn the receiving energy.

The first thing I want you to know and remember is that there IS divine flow in life. We find that delicious sweet flow when we trust. We trust that the universe has our back. We trust our own deep knowing and intuition. Receiving is the same as flowing. Flowing with life, flowing with the mystery. We understand that there will always be mystery in life and we come to love that sweet mystery. Rather than being afraid of the mystery—the unknown—we learn to embrace it. And then life, our lives, begin to flow. And the more we trust that flow, the more our lives flow, and the more life flows, the more we receive and want to receive. It is a wonderful cycle that just keeps feeding upon itself, in such a good way.

Of course, there are times that don't seem as if there is any divine flow in life. But trust me, there is. We often feel there is no flow because we have temporarily lost our way. We have forgotten the wild, holy, feminine creatures that we are. We have forgotten that we are divinely connected to the earth, the moon, to nature . . . that we are of the earth.

We cannot find flow and fluidity in our lives without opening to receiving and opening to surrendering. Does that scare you? It can be frightening to think of receiving and surrendering. Both require being open and vulnerable. They require that we give up our ideas of control. And, oh, that is so hard for some of us. For even though we really don't have control, we mistakenly think we do. And this "mistaken" thought can bring us so much pain. Much more pain than relinquishing control and moving toward flow and surrender and receiving.

Receiving is a little bit like surrender. We begin by accepting the fact that life doesn't have to be so hard. We don't have to strive so hard for what we want. The universe wants us to have what we need and want. The universe has our back. This is where the surrender and trust comes in. Yes, some work is always required. But life doesn't have to be constant pushing and pulling to get where we want to go. How much ease are you willing to allow yourself as you move through life? Wouldn't it feel good to slow down just a little, to not always feel that life is difficult and hard, to find sweet ease within your life, within your effort? It can be that way. The more we slow down and listen, the more we feel fulfilled by our desired accomplishments.

As you embrace your wild feminine energy, you will be guided into ways of moving and living with ease and grace. You are here to receive all the goodness, all the abundance of the earth. You don't have to do anything to receive that goodness. When you understand and believe this, you will begin to find more ease in everything you do. Because you are not striving to prove yourself. There is nothing to prove. You are good enough just as you are.

Your wild feminine self knows that we are cyclical beings. And, just as in nature, we have times to produce and times to savor and times to replenish. All are equally important. And we follow these patterns by learning to open to receive.

Think of it like this. Receiving is as simple as inhaling. Just as you simply inhale in order to take air into your lungs for survival, you can inhale from your world what you need and desire. Don't make it so hard. Trust that the universe is looking out for you. Remember that the universe has its own timeline. We are not in control of when things will happen or even how they will happen. But we are in control of how we feel and how we respond to life.

As I said earlier, receiving is trusting. How would your life feel if you just trusted that your life is flowing the way it is meant to? Wouldn't you feel more ease, more grace? To have this trust and this receiving, you must live in the present moment. Know that what you need will come to you when the time is right. And know that where you are right now is where you are meant to be. There is a gentle surrender to this. And life begins to feel easier. When we make our choices and decisions from this place, we have a bone-deep knowing that we are moving in the right direction. That we are living authentically. And when we live authentically, we are able to receive. Receive from the universe, receive from others, and receive from ourselves. Slowing down enough to see what we really need and want.

This receiving takes place even when we are working toward something and it makes the doing easier and lighter. The doing is not filled with anxiety or stress. The doing is in a place of grace, of lightness, of pleasure. That's when our lives begin to feel as if they are flowing. So sweet.

We think of receiving as being in flow. That makes it a little more palatable to some. When we are open to receiving in all its ways and forms, we move with the stream of life rather than trying to paddle upstream. And what a difference that makes. When we open to receive, everything feels lighter.

In what areas of your life are you paddling upstream? Desperately trying to make something (or someone) happen, something that might be totally out of your control. How would your life look and feel if you allowed yourself to just flow? To receive by accepting that this is how your life is now and gently flowing into what is next. This isn't the same as resigning yourself to something. Not at all. This is just knowing that life moves at its own pace and we take steps to move ourselves toward what we want and need, but we take those steps in trust that everything will come as it will.

So we're still doing (at times), we're still moving forward, but our perspective, our attitude, is different. We feel at ease. We may even feel joy.

Which brings me to another idea. With all the angst-ridden striving that you sometimes do, are you striving and moving toward those things and ideas that you really desire? Or are the things you're moving toward someone else's idea of what you need or who you need to be? When we open ourselves to receiving and live within our feminine wildness, we begin to choose authentic ways of living our lives. We want to move toward what moves us. In other words, we begin to choose those things that create a spark in us. We choose ideas and desires that bring us passion. And when we do that, any efforting seems to have ease within it, seems to be filled with grace and desire. So, yes, we effort, we work toward something, but it is toward something we desire and, because of this, it doesn't seem like work. It might be difficult, but it is sustaining. It makes us feel good, not tired and worn out.

For many of us, this is a whole new way to move through life. What if every day when you got out of bed, you were excited about your activities? This is receiving. This is opening up to trust. This is flow.

And as we find those pleasurable ways of moving through our day, we also take time to slow down. We take time to replenish ourselves. To listen to what our bodies and our spirits need. This is a big part of receiving. Taking time to breathe, to meditate, to just dream, we find that receiving and trusting is easier. We begin to see how the tapestry of our lives weaves itself together. If we are constantly busy, constantly striving, we can't even see a piece of the cloth, much less the entire tapestry. Seeing this tapestry of our lives, seeing how it all comes together in ways we never imagine possible, helps us to open to receive even more. It is all a beautiful cycle.

Some questions to ponder and, hopefully, journal with:

- Where in my life am I "doing" too much or striving too hard?
- Where in my life might I choose to slow down and just notice?
- How does flow look to me?
- Where in my life do I have flow right now?
- How does it feel?
- How do I feel when I accept help? Is it easy for me?

Short meditation for receiving

Take a comfortable seat or lie down. Begin with a couple of deep full inhales and long sighing exhales through your mouth. As you do this, feel your body softening with each breath. Feel softness in your face and shoulders. Begin to let your breath find its natural rhythm. Think of your breath as a river that is flowing through you, touching every cell in your body. As this river of breath flows, notice how it eases tension in your body.

Imagine your body softly opening to receive this river of your breath. And as you softly open, feel your river of breath expanding. Feel it flowing so easily that you begin to just get lost in the rhythm. Maybe this flow makes you feel like rocking or moving gently as you sit. Do what feels right to you. Open yourself to receive any movement that is needed. Open yourself to receive any emotions that might be arising.

Now, if it feels right, bring to mind an area in your life where you believe you are struggling too much. An area that just feels as if you are constantly pushing and pushing to have it be what you want it to be. As you bring this to mind, allow your river of breath to flow into this idea, this place. Use your imagination as much as you need or want. Breathe into this struggle and begin to feel a soft flow develop within your struggle. As you do this, notice the softness that will begin to rise within you as you continue to think of this struggle. Allow yourself to soften even more around this struggle. How does it feel now?

Maybe you ask yourself is this something I really want? Me, not someone else? And if so, how might I make this more pleasurable? How might the moving toward it bring me joy? Can I begin to lighten up my struggle and trust that what I want is moving toward me? How might I trust that what I want wants me?

Sit with these ideas and just breathe into them for as long as you'd like. Feel these thoughts and ideas in your body rather than in your head. What sorts of feelings and emotions appear as you think about allowing more flow within this part of your life? Of inviting in more receptivity and pleasure around this idea?

When you feel ready, bring one hand to your belly and one hand to your heart. Say to yourself, "I am open to receive. I trust that I can live my life in flow with ease and grace. I embrace and honor my wild feminine self and trust her to show me how to receive." Take another deep breath in and slowly, very slowly, exhale through your mouth with a sigh. Slowly open your eyes, move your body just a little, and when you're ready move back into your day.

As you move through your day, notice when you feel in flow. Notice the sensations and feelings in your body when you feel open to receiving. Not just receiving from others, but receiving from nature, from the universe. Do you notice that you feel more in flow with your life when you are open in heart and body to receive life just as it is happening in this moment, even if what is happening is not what you want exactly? When we are with whatever is happening, just as it is, our lives continue to flow. We can feel the ease and grace within the difficulty. It feels good and right and we notice this sensation of goodness in our bodies.

Chapter 7

Gratitude and Abundance

> "I ask you again, if you have not been enchanted by this adventure—your life—what would do it for you?" - Mary Oliver

Gratitude is a ritual, or a practice, that changes our lives by changing our mental outlook. This has been proven by brain studies now (if that gives you more reason to practice). I use gratitude practices throughout my day, both written and verbally.

When I first began to practice "written" gratitude lists on a daily basis, it was in the throes of my life as I knew it turning upside down. My husband was no longer even trying to give up alcohol, our marriage was dissolving, and I was in despair, losing everything I knew and loved.

Trying to pull myself up, even just a little, I hoped, I began making lengthy gratitude lists everyday—at least ten things. So often I would have to search and search, and lots of times they were very simple things: I am grateful for my kitties, for a soft bed, for my students, etc. As the weeks went by, I found my mood gradually improving. Finding things to be grateful for became easier. But maybe most importantly, I began to find my own inner strength again, my resilience.

I began to realize that just by taking tiny steps every day I was feeling stronger. I trusted myself more. My wild feminine was stirring again, eager to be honored and "let loose."

So I firmly believe, for so many reasons, that gratitude is a practice to bring all of us back to our wildness, our power. And it is such a simple practice. It's important to remember that gratitude is not just words you write. Gratitude must be felt viscerally.

I invite you to stop right now, this moment. Take three deep breaths with me, letting your exhales be a nice long sigh. Now think of three things that you are grateful for in this moment—small is good. Maybe one of them is gratitude for your own breath. Just whatever first pops into your head. No right or wrong. And now, take two or three deep breaths again. How do you feel in this moment? Maybe a little calmer? A little sweet joy in your body? Maybe a little smile on your face?

Moments throughout your day that can be a signal to pause and be grateful are:

* Sitting at a stop light or in traffic
* Sitting down to eat
* Whenever your phone rings

You could also set reminders on your phone for every few hours. There are many times throughout our day that would benefit from checking in with ourselves, our gratitude, and our breath. Give it a try and see for yourself.

Doesn't gratitude just feel good? When we find ourselves being grateful, we feel as if we are glowing, like there is a sun inside us just glowing outward. Gratitude will change our lives. And it works quickly to change our perspective of how we look at our lives and how we see the people in our lives. If you do nothing else to make yourself happier, gratitude is the one thing I would recommend. It is that powerful.

You've already heard me say how powerful our words are. They are spells. When we feel grateful, not only do we use powerful words but those words elicit a feeling in our bodies as all powerful words should do. So gratitude is a feeling, a deep feeling, rather than just an expression of words. And that is how it changes our lives and our perspective.

When we make gratitude a practice, it becomes easier and easier to tap into these exquisite feelings. We begin to change the patterns and pathways in our brains. And we begin to WANT to feel the sensations and feelings we associate with gratitude. We then begin to look for things to be grateful for, because it just seems natural. Because it has, in fact, become your nature to be grateful.

And when it is our nature to be grateful, we are content, we are happy, and we trust and know that we will receive more things to be grateful for. It is this beautiful cycle that just keeps repeating itself.

A good way to begin practicing gratitude is to establish a daily practice. As with any other practice we have talked about, consistency is key. And I believe you will find that a gratitude practice is fun. The beauty is that you will begin to feel a difference with your first session.

The beauty of a consistent practice is that you will begin to move through your day looking for things to be grateful for. In my life and practice, I call this looking for the magic every day. It is a wonderful feeling at the end of the day to tally up all the magic you saw and felt that day, and to be grateful for it.

As your gratitude practice grows and expands, you will notice that you have so much abundance. Nothing has really changed in your life other than you are NOTICING all that you have. And as you begin to notice, you see even more and more. In a few weeks, you will see that your mindset, your perspective, is beginning to change.

Research shows us that gratitude makes us more positive and happy. It also makes us more resilient and trusting. But we don't need research to tell us that because we can see it in our own lives.

As I said earlier, consistency is the biggest key factor. But another important key is that we must FEEL our gratitude. To reap its benefits, gratitude must be felt in our bodies. It must be more than just words we speak. There we are again, that embodiment thing (smile). I told you how important embodiment was in this process of embracing our wildness.

How does gratitude feel in your body? How do you experience gratitude? Are you good at being grateful? One of the ways to begin to notice the feelings of gratitude is to spend a few moments thinking of something that you are grateful for. When we take moments to think about what we are grateful for, we want to pause long enough to sit with those words. We want to ask, "Why am I grateful for this?" And then, "How does this (person, thing, or event for which I am grateful) make me feel?" "What does it bring to my life?" Focusing on the "why" of our gratitude helps us to begin the "feeling" of gratitude. As you sit with these thoughts, notice sensations in your body—maybe in your heart space, maybe in your belly. Often, a warmth begins to spread throughout your body. You may have a feeling of your heart opening, having less constriction, as if your body has just taken a big sigh. It is important as we begin a gratitude practice to notice these feelings in our bodies. This is how gratitude feels. Whatever you feel, stay there with it for a few moments. By doing this, you are creating new neural pathways. And this is how we begin to change our attitude. And that feeling will stay with us for a while, maybe making us feel soft and tender and loving. Good feelings!

Even if you're a little skeptical, isn't it worth playing the game just to see, out of curiosity, if it works for you? If you play this "magical gratitude" game consistently, I promise you will see a difference in how you look at your life and in how much abundance you have and continue to gather. Because as we focus on abundance and gratitude we continue to receive more abundance. Remember we said earlier that what we focus on grows. This is a fact of life. So why don't we focus on gratitude and abundance as opposed to negativity and lack?

I'll share with you some of the little things that I do to remind myself to be present and grateful. Take what works for you and know that, as you practice, it will soon become just second nature. And that is a beautiful thing!

After doing my morning energy meditation and stretching, I wash the sleep from my eyes, asking the water element to take away my energies from the night, leaving me with fresh eyes. I always say thank you for a good night's sleep and for a brand new day. Just thinking this makes me feel fully present as I rinse my eyes and then dab on some essential oils. Washing my face is something I would do anyway, but I have added presence and gratitude to it.

I love to keep a gratitude journal daily. In the beginning, years ago, I had a journal dedicated specifically to gratitude.

Now, I keep a little journal by my bed in which I list my gratitude, but I also use it for sketches and short journaling practices in the morning. I do think that it is very important to WRITE your gratitude lists at least once a day. And, hopefully, you make mental gratitude lists throughout your day.

So back to my practice. Usually, while still in bed in the morning, with a cup of steaming coffee, I write three to four things I am grateful for. I usually also write why I am grateful for them. And I usually write "thank you."

I also do this same practice most nights just before I go to sleep. I believe it sets us up for a brighter, happier tomorrow when the last thing we are thinking about is the beautiful magic that happened to us that day.

Remember, you can list as many things as you'd like. But I always try to list different things every time! The key is to stretch yourself. We all have so much abundance in our lives. And your gratitude lists can be the tiniest little things. Remember it is all about what makes you happy, what feels good to you. No one else has to read your list. Make it very personal. That's where those warm feelings come in, when it means something to YOU.

What I have found is that by writing my gratitude out twice a day I begin to really look for things that are magically different as I move through my day. This is why I call my list (especially my evening list) my magical list for the day. And it might only be one thing but it is something special for that day. And it may be extremely tiny and insignificant to someone else. Sometimes on my run I will see a beautiful purple flower growing right up out of the sand on the beach. That is magical and brightens my day. But I might not have even noticed it if I had not been present and looking for the magic that day.

As you practice gratitude, dive deep into the details, the sometimes messiness. Gratitude is not always joyful appreciation. Often it is gratitude for the mundane, the ordinary. Just as often it is gratitude for the pain and sadness, simply gratitude that you feel, gratitude for your humanness. Don't sugarcoat it. Make it real and raw and, most of all, yours. And if you can't find any gratitude, just write how you feel. All of it.

One of the most beautiful benefits of gratitude is that it brings me into the present moment. And that is where we live our lives. It brings us into the moment when we are thinking about what we are grateful for and giving it feeling, and it also brings us into the present moment so often throughout the day because we are looking for things to be grateful for. As our perspective changes our radar begins to pick up on things we may never have noticed before. That is being present. That is happiness. And, for me, the biggest reason for practicing gratitude.

So why not give it a try? You don't have to have a fancy journal. Just a piece of paper will do, or you could keep notes on your phone. Set aside time in the morning and maybe again at night to write down three things for which you are grateful. And write just a word or two about why you are grateful for that. Do this every day and see what happens. Be curious. I think you will notice even on the first day that you start your day with a positive outlook after just spending a few moments in gratitude.

Before I write, I sit in stillness and take three or four deep full breaths. This just helps to settle me into my body which is where I want to be as I think of gratitude. Taking my awareness into my belly or my heart space. And then I take a moment to thoughtfully write.

Make it something that works for you. Maybe after breakfast is better for you. Though I do recommend a little bit of gratitude time before you truly begin your day. And a little bit of gratitude time before you go to sleep. If you don't want to write again in the evening, just before you drift off to sleep take a few moments to mentally list two or three things that you are grateful for that happened that day. There are times, of course, that we may really have to search for something. But that's okay. Just find some tiny little thing—maybe a nice hot shower—that you can be grateful for. Most days will be easier, I promise.

Here are some examples of my gratitude/mindful journaling:

Right now, here . . . just finished a short run and a sweet dip in the ocean. Bathed in the energy of Mama moon, Father sun, and Mama ocean, grounding, energizing, and delicious. Perfect start to my day. FaceTime with J to start day. Cup of coffee. Life is good. Thank you.

Here, right now . . . saw a crane by the river as we sat eating dinner and drinking wine. "Erik" from Nicaragua who looks just like a young Dustin Hoffman . . . having coffee . . . then we'll walk the street again and see all the art . . . gratitude for this amazing day.

This moment, right now . . . coffee in hand, feeling peaceful, looking forward to my day. Intention to be wholehearted in all of it today—passion as well as ease—magic . . . life is good, my wild feminine self is alive, very much alive today. I want to feel ecstatic today. Thank you.

Here, this moment . . . melancholy maybe . . . a little low . . . grateful for a big mug of JOY filled with coffee . . . makes me smile . . . grateful for that today. I will eat better and move more (smile) . . . grateful that I can celebrate Christmas, though I will miss three of the people I loved most, yet I know they are with me in spirit. I want to embrace all these feelings—sadness, joy, and gratitude.

Right now . . . feeling quiet . . . asking my deep wild feminine "what's next?" Waiting for answers . . . okay with not knowing because right now is good . . . want to stay here awhile and just be content . . . here . . . sweetness and some nostalgia. Thank you.

Here . . . coffee in my Joy mug . . . Gracie on my lap . . . lying under a feeling of contentment . . . and under the softest warm blanket (though I only want it for its soft touch—don't need it for warmth) (smile).

Here . . . this morning . . . giving myself permission to feel it all . . . sweet morning . . . sipping coffee . . . feeling a little anxious even as I woke up . . . grateful for pen and paper and words though sometimes I have feelings with no words . . . right now, here . . . holding many feelings with no words to describe . . . I am holy and fierce . . . and sometimes sad and afraid . . . and it is okay. It is okay. Reminding myself that no matter what, I am wildly free to be me . . . to be me . . . whether it is chaotic and messy, or teary and sad, or wild and screaming, or peacefully breathing . . . free to be me . . . and I am grateful for all that.

Chapter 8

Everyday Magic

"Where there is a woman there is magic."
– Ntozake Shange

"I don't want realism. I want magic!"
– Tennessee Williams, A *Streetcar Named Desire*

Magic. Just hearing the word makes you tingle a little, doesn't it? Magic intrigues us, maybe makes us smile. And maybe the word makes some laugh, as if it is absurd. But trust me, believing in magic and looking for magic is holy. And it will change your life.

What pictures do you conjure up when you hear the word magic? As children, we all believed in magic. We had vivid imaginations. Sadly, as we grow older, we begin to lose touch with our magic. Our world doesn't seem quite so sparkly, does it?

Recapturing my magic created vivid moments in my life. By looking for magic I began to see that indeed the world is filled with magic and wonder, wonder that we miss if we are rushing nonstop from one to-do to the next. Magic needs the fluidity and receptivity of our wild feminine energy, our energy that is able to see beyond the ordinary or maybe underneath the ordinary.

The phrase "extraordinary lies just beneath the skin of ordinary" has stuck closely with me. It is so true. We just need to look a little deeper to find all the wonder, the magic, the extraordinary that is right there in front of us.

You are the magic

Do you ever feel that the magic has gone out of your life? Or maybe that you've never felt that magic? I'm here to remind you that you are the magic. Magic is always inside you. Sometimes we bury it or it gets buried by life itself, but it is always there, waiting to be revived.

When we unearth our magic, we feel sparkly, glowing, passionate. It brings a whole new quality to our lives. Our magic is a connection to all the elements—earth, air, water, fire, and spirit.

When we remember our magic, we see everything with fresh, new eyes. It's almost like looking through the eyes of a child. We begin to see everything and everyone as wondrous, mysterious, intriguing. Magic is curiosity, wonder, anticipation. When was the last time you felt this way about your life, your relationships, your work?

Living from our wild feminine nature, we are in touch with our magic, with our ability to intuitively see and feel. Our wild self is magic herself, so why would we not be able to draw magic toward us? We seduce magic. And with this magic we create our lives.

When we begin to live with and embrace our wild feminine, we get in touch with our magic. The wildness of our divine feminine is always magic. Intuition is magic and our wild self is intuition. When we find our magic, we are present, divinely aware. We get lost in all our senses. Magic is visceral. Magic is juicy. When we feel our magic, we are in the flow of life. We know that we can create anything we want. With magic, we open ourselves up to receive. With magic, we know and trust our intuition.

Knowing and trusting yourself is how you re-create your magic. Knowing you are way more than enough just as you are. Knowing that when you are authentic—in all your messiness, your wonder, your ecstasy, your sorrow—that is when you are magic.

So how do we begin to engage with our magic? All new adventures, or journeys, are begun with deep, full belly breaths, right into the heart of our feminine wildness.

Finding our magic meditation

Take three deep breaths with me now, with your hands touching your belly. With your eyes closed, set an intention to open yourself up to magic—your own divine magic and the magic all around you. Breathe deeply until you can feel yourself opening to your magic. Maybe it feels like a soft fluttering in your belly, maybe like a ribbon of anticipation. All is welcome.

With hands still on your belly, ask your wild spirit to open your heart, your body, and your spirit to the magic that is you. Feel your unique power, your unique energy. Breathe deeply, swaying your body. Imagine a bright red orange glow in your belly—a fire of magic. As you breathe into it, feel the flames growing brighter and moving through your body. With every inhale your fire grows brighter and with every exhale your fire of magic moves through your body. Feel your magic. When you are ready, open your eyes and take your magic out into your world.

Once you have opened your heart, body, and spirit to feel magic, here's the way to bring magic to you every day. Look for it. Sounds simple but it works. In your journal or on your calendar, you are going to write down one magical thing that you saw, heard, felt that day. Very much like your gratitude practice. In fact, gratitude and magic have a lot in common. Remember, magic is in the simple things. It is our awareness of the simple things, our presence to them that makes it all magical. Because we are able to see the wonder within the simple. "Extraordinary lies just beneath the skin of ordinary" exemplifies magic to me. The magic is there waiting for us. We must see beneath the ordinary.

Most of the time magic goes unnoticed. I've been jotting down daily magic for five years now and this alone has brought me much joy. And the best part is that, over time, it has encouraged me to be present as I move through my day. You can't spot magic and wonder unless you are here, not hundreds of years away in your head.

This is some of the "magic" I have seen or felt daily: a rainbow covering the entire sky, a tiny little bird that lights on a leaf of a bush, a crane standing solid guard in my yard, fog deep over the ocean, my lover's touch, a smile from a stranger, a truly decadent piece of cake. These were all special to me because I immersed myself in them, no hurry, savoring, feeling, being touched by them, lingering with them.

And when I recorded them by writing them in my journal, I re-lived the feelings again. This is how we make new neural pathways which set us up for more magic.

I also found that knowing I wanted to write a magical occurrence or "sighting" every day, I would spend my day looking for it. In other words, I would move through my day open, present, and with an attitude of wonder, just knowing that something magical would happen. And it always does. What we look for and anticipate we find. So let's look for magic and wonder, shall we? And just as with gratitude, dive deep. Don't just see the surface magic. See the magic that is also beneath your sadness, your anger.

Some journaling prompts for you:

- ✶ What makes me feel magical?
- ✶ What can I get lost in?
- ✶ How do I access and bring forth my divine power?
- ✶ How does magic feel in my body?

Chapter 9

Everyday Creativity

"If you're going to dance, then darling, make the world spin." – Madalyn Beck

I would not have survived the past few years, or maybe even my life, without creativity. When I give myself up to the muse, to creativity, I begin to feel whole again. In a short while I feel juicy. Creativity is the wild feminine. The wild feminine is creativity. When we create, we have to let go, we have to be receptive, just opening ourselves up and trusting.

Creativity helps us connect to our wild feminine, that raw, real part of ourselves. That is why creating often feels so scary. It is scary to let go and trust. But that is what the divine feminine asks of us—to trust, to believe, and not worry about the outcome.

Who me? Creative? Sadly, I have heard so many women say those exact words. We are women. We are all creative. All of us. Repeat after me, I am creative, I am creative. In our wild femininity we are creators of everything and maybe our greatest creation is our own lives. How have you been creating your life lately?

Whether you write or paint or cook or play music, notice how in the flow you are. Notice how juicy and ripe you begin to feel—as if life is just oozing out of you. You feel as if it's difficult to contain, as if you're ready to burst open. This is creativity. This is passion.

This is how all your life can feel. You can feel this aliveness in every facet of your life. The wild feminine, our wild feminine, takes us there. Creating, we are in the present moment, just here, now, life is sweet and flowing. Sometimes, often, we have to trust the process to get to that flow, that juiciness. But it is always there waiting for us.

Yes, you are creative. We are all creative. Our wild spirit thrives on creativity. By her very nature, the wild feminine creates. She creates everything, and everything is a creation.

As humans, we are meant to create. When we create, we use our imaginations. We let go of control and, maybe best of all, we learn to be in the "not-knowing" without freaking out, because when we are creating anything, we have to trust. We don't know where it is going and creativity is not something that can be planned.

Please remember that creativity is not about producing. It is about the process. We cannot come to wild, magical creativity worrying about the end product, the outcome, because we really don't know what that will look like. What we do is come to the process of creating every day and just be curious as to what shows up.

Like many things we've already talked about, creativity is a practice. The best way to reap its benefits and free our spirits is to come to it every day. Whether we feel creative or inspired or not. We just show up and see what happens. And often, something beautiful happens.

Your muse or spirit guides your creative practice. So we must learn to give her the freedom to play. As we do in other areas of our lives, we open ourselves up to receive her guidance. Yes, it is very scary to face that blank page, or that blank canvas, but we learn to trust the process.

And most of all, we know that we are doing this for ourselves. We are giving our spirits expression. As we delve into our creativity—whatever it is—we learn about ourselves. But even better, our expression of creativity brings us joy. It gives a spark to our lives. Our spirits, our bodies, our wild selves are begging for expression. We need this. You need this. And yes, you are creative.

Let's begin by defining creativity. What does creativity mean to you? What are some things you have done that make you lose all track of time? Keep you totally absorbed in the moment?

All things are creative. Our lives are our greatest artwork. We create everyday, whether we call it that or not. Gardening, baking bread, creating a delicious dinner, a project at work or school, writing, painting, sketching, arranging cut flowers, decorating your home, creating sacred space—all are creative acts. What can you add to these?

Creativity of all kinds sparks joy and happiness even if what we are expressing is our anger or sadness. Creativity is an amazing way to express our anger and sadness. The end result is always joy and peacefulness. Wholeness. So isn't that worth a try? Keep in mind that YOU ARE CREATIVE.

Have you ever felt that something was missing from your life? You couldn't really put your finger on it, but something just didn't feel right. Something was missing. That something is creativity! Creativity is your unique way of expressing who you are in what you do. Creativity expresses itself in myriad ways. Think of creativity as an expression rather than a product. The product, if there is one, isn't important. So think for a moment. In what ways do you express yourself? Maybe by cooking a succulent chocolate cake, dancing a tantalizing tango, growing plants or creating a garden, throwing paint on canvas, or just wildly dancing around the room to express your happiness. In what ways are you creative in everyday life?

The problem is that most of us believe that creativity must produce a "product," something that looks good or professional, maybe something valuable that can be bought and sold. Most of us fear creativity because we are attached to the outcome. These thoughts stop so many of us from opening ourselves to the joy and satisfaction of creating, and these thoughts are totally false. But we believe them because we live in a culture that honors productivity above everything else. But that is not creativity at all. Creativity is the expression of your heart, your body, your spirit, into your creation, whatever that creation might be. There is no expectation of an end result.

I invite you to begin to think of a creative practice as a spiritual practice. Not something that has to be taken so seriously but a means to let your spirit sing. Creativity is a way to speak what's in your heart, body, and soul. Creativity is intuitive. It is a way to get to know your true essence and a way to engage your true essence. Creativity is a beautiful way to navigate your way through the hills and valleys of your life. And, above all, like everything else we have talked about, it is a practice. A sweet, joyful practice.

Giving myself permission to do things badly has been the one thing that has allowed my creativity to come out to play whenever I wanted to play! You'll be amazed how exciting it finally feels to say, "Okay, so what if it's not the best writing I can do. I'm gonna do it anyway." There is such freedom to those words and that attitude. I no longer have to do it perfectly (if I felt it had to be perfect, I would never put pen to paper). And I imagine you are the same way. I give myself the freedom to do it badly, to just play, to have fun. It is not serious anymore.

We come to the creative process, invited by our muse, to just express ourselves. As we face the blank canvas, or the blank page, or the mass of clay or glass, we have no idea what we are going to create. Once again, we come to that trust and surrendering, surrendering to the process of our own creativity. We silence our inner critic, those limiting beliefs, so that we can allow ourselves to just flow.

It may feel quite sticky at first. But the more we do it, the more we start to feel alive. Like, yes, this is what I need to do.

Creativity itself, of any kind, creates a feeling of aliveness—a feeling of joy for life. We feel that we are able to fully express ourselves, our feelings, and the good part is that we never have to share it with anyone if we don't want to. This creativity is for you alone, for your well-being, for your beautiful wild feminine self who MUST create. In order to be happy, to feel fulfilled, she needs to create.

Most importantly, creativity should be playful. As you come to creativity practice, especially if you're a little intimidated, I invite you to just think of this as playtime. Because that is what it is. How do you like to play? A way to just let go, to be spontaneous, to just play with whatever medium you are playing with, and remember that medium might be in the kitchen or with your plants. Creativity is expression of yourself, of your spirit. Think of it as "playtime" that has profound effects on our lives and our feelings. Because creativity encourages us to dive deep into ourselves, into our shadows, to feel free.

If we take ourselves too seriously our muse will never come to play. And our wild feminine muse likes to play. She never takes herself too seriously. Most of all, she is constantly changing. And she is spontaneous always. She wants to play, to take risks, to be fearless, to laugh at herself. She likes to stand naked to the world—to show herself in all her vibrancy. To be known.

But if we strive for perfection, she is sure to leave. She absolutely hates perfection. It has no place in creativity—ever. Because perfection is something that can never be achieved. It is only your inner critic, your limiting belief, raising its ugly head.

So are you ready to play a little? Without giving it a whole lot of thought, what first comes to mind when you think of playing? Is there something that you've always wanted to try? Or is there something you used to do as a child that you might enjoy trying again? Keep in mind that this is play. Creativity is play; play is creativity. Please don't take it too seriously and don't take yourself too seriously.

This is a time for exploration and curiosity. What might you be curious about? If you are just beginning your creative journey, it makes sense to explore lots of different things. You may surprise yourself with what you enjoy creating. Maybe you even join a group or a class.

Remember through this exploration that you are awakening your wild feminine self. Start by having a conversation with her. What intrigues her? What turns her on?

If you listen closely she will tell you. Listen to your body, listen to your heart.

Creativity and sexual energy are one and the same. Did you hear me? Creativity = sexuality. Sexuality = creativity. It is all the same energy. And both of these energies arise from your sacral chakra. These energies are your Shakti—your wild feminine divine energy. This is why it is so important to express your creativity. This is YOU. YOU are creative, you are a sexual creature. These two energies play so well with each other. And all of this takes us right back to desire.

When we are creating, we feel our sexual energy. When we feel our sexual energy, we often want to create. Maybe this is one reason we fear our creativity just a little. Feeling our sexual energy grow, flourish, and expand is often a little scary if we are not used to it. But this sexual feeling, this sexual energy, is our life force. Without it we are not living the fullness that is available to us. This sexual energy, this creative force, is our aliveness. It is what makes us curious, brings us passion for everything, helps us to feel delight, and enables us to see the magic in the mundane. All of which are a zest for living.

So maybe all this talk of sexual energy and zest for life has you excited to begin your creative journey. Just think of it as an exploration to see what makes you feel juicy, to see what makes you feel delicious. That's all it need be.

When we are creating, we are in the flow. Time passes quickly and we are not even aware of it. It feels as if time has slowed. We are totally immersed in what we are doing. When we are creating, we are totally embodied. (There is that embodiment thing again.) And this embodiment is one of the reasons creativity is so important to our well-being, to our happiness, and to our mental health. Creativity, in all its forms, is vital to our wild feminine nature. As you embrace your own version of creativity, you will feel alive. And that feeling keeps you coming back. You take a feeling and create something out of it. How beautiful is that?

There are so many ways to create. Keep in mind that creating is just expressing your true self. What does your true self want or need to express? Give her the freedom to be spontaneous. This will bring out the child in you, which is a great place to start. Just letting the child in you play.

I ask that you give yourself permission to do it badly. Really badly. Know that your best creativity emerges from doing it imperfectly, as do SO many things in life! Splendidly imperfect! Don't you just love that phrase? It is so appropriate for all us splendidly imperfect wild women. What better way to be!

I once read that a writer is someone who wrote this morning. Not someone who wrote a book, or someone who has been published, or someone who knows grammar perfectly. But someone who simply wrote "this" morning. What an inspiration that was for me! Yes, I am a writer! To me it means you can BE something by DOING it. But the most important part is that you don't have to do it a certain way. It doesn't have to be the best, or the most inspirational, but it does have to be done. It can be messy, sloppy, scary, but that's okay. This gives me freedom. I feel as if I have wings and I want that for you! You, too, have wings of creativity to fly.

Go ahead. Try it for yourself. Substitute whatever your greatest desire is. What do you want to be?

A runner is someone who runs. A writer is someone who writes. A painter is someone who paints. A speaker is someone who speaks. A chef is someone who cooks. A dancer is someone who dances. See? And did you notice that there is a period after each one? Nothing else. A dancer is someone who dances, period, not dances well or dances the tango, etc.

Now are you inspired to just do it in any way that feels good? The joy comes in the creating, not in the perfect product. So let your joy pour out of you. Open yourself up to creating badly. You'll find that you ARE a dancer, a chef, an artist.

If, like many, you are not sure where your creative muse is leading you, let's start with a couple of playful activities and see what happens.

Drawing/Painting—bringing out the Picasso in you!

I like to think of painting as just spreading colors around on a canvas or page. I couldn't live without tubs of markers, crayons, colored pencils, pens, and tubes of paint. It makes me happy looking at them all scattered around or running over their tubs. If you want to stimulate your muse, bring out the crayons, paint, and paper. Remember when you used to finger paint? Actually, finger painting is a great place to start. Pick the colors you like most, squeeze a little onto your paper or canvas, and begin to spread it around. Play. Feel the texture of the paint on your fingers and hands. Feel the texture of the paper underneath your hands. See the bright colors moving around. Smell the paint. Notice anything here? Creating goes hand in hand with sensuality—you are using all your senses to bring yourself into this moment. And that's why/when you just get lost in it.

Go back to your childhood days when a blank, white sheet of paper inspired you to draw circles, lines, flowers. You wanted to fill up every nook and crevice. Nothing else mattered at that moment.

If it feels right, pick up a paint brush and just begin to make some strokes. Spontaneous play, remember? When you feel you've done enough, let it dry and come back to it later. I promise you, it will always look better when you come back. Then maybe you'd like to put a few marks on your paper with a black or white pen. Marks don't have to be anything special, just whatever mark appeals to you at the moment. I like to put words on my paintings. I often journal my feelings and paint right over them, especially my feelings of anger or pain. Very therapeutic. Let your intuition guide you and play, play, play.

Whenever your critic raises her ugly head, just say, "It's okay, I'll listen to you later. Right now, I'm just playing and I can do it as badly as I want." Keep giving yourself permission.

How do you feel?

Writing

Writing is the creative way I connect with myself. It is one of the ways I listen to what my body is saying to me. And I believe that writing works this way for everyone. Writing brings us closer to ourselves, to really knowing who we are. Writing is a way of exploring ourselves—our darkness, our shadows, as well as everything that lights us up. The more we write, the more we learn, the more authentic we become. But many women tell me that they just can't sit down and write. They don't know what to say.

So I want you to remember that EVERYONE can write. The kind of writing I am talking about is what we sometimes call "free writing." Throwing your thoughts and feelings onto paper without any editing or correction. Just write without lifting the pen off the paper. And it is powerful. It is a powerful way to connect with yourself, to find out who you are and what you need. Especially with practice.

I wanted to share a few of my writings with you so you see how they can look. I often use prompts. Writing prompts are just a way to begin your writing as you face that blank page. You write the prompt and go from there.

Keep coming back to the prompt when you feel you've run out of words. Prompts are delicious ways to spark my creativity, which eventually drops me into my authenticity. Prompts such as "Right now . . . here . . ." or "I want to tell you" or "I feel . . ." In these writings, I was using the prompts "my mind wants me to know . . ." "my heart wants me to know . . ." "my belly wants me to know . . ." I use these types of prompts often. And usually just write for a few minutes.

3/3 My head wants me to know that sometimes it is wild and crazy yet it is always, it says, doing what it thinks it should to keep me safe. My head apologizes for wanting to be in control. My heart wants me to know I am love. That my heart is filled with sweetness and sorrow (a mixture of both), and from that rawness it wants me to feel loved and to spread love. My heart loves to be open and it doesn't even mind being vulnerable. It wants to remind me of that. My belly wants to tell me that I am full of life, that passion moves through my belly like a fire, hot and beautiful. And my fire is always ready to spread and grow even bigger. My belly wants to tell me to trust this fire, this passion, that it is true.

3/7 My head wants me to know it feels satisfyingly quiet this morning. A sense of peace rather than scurrying around. Ahhh . . . my heart wants me to know it feels nourished. Lots of early morning heartwarming snuggles with J this morning. He brought me a sweet roll. My heart feels expansive. My belly says it also feels satisfied as well as powerful today. All the delicious lovemaking last evening and this morning with J has made my heart and my belly feel happy, satisfied, loved, and cherished. Good start to the day, belly says.

11/3 Head, heart, and belly seem to all be on the same wavelength today. I believe starting my morning off with my lover helps that. The snuggling, feeling his body pressed next to mine, heals my head, heart, and belly. Funny, isn't it, how feeling loved, cherished, and desired also makes you feel powerful. I feel powerfully feminine in my wildness today.

12/20 My head wants to tell me that it feels crazy and chaotic today. Anxiety underlies all this. My head says it really wants calm and quiet. My heart wants me to know that it feels melancholy today . . . a little vulnerable . . . missing what used to be and so uncertain of what is to come. My heart wants me know that she is also holding just a little bit of gratitude for what we do have, how far we have come. My belly wants me to know that all of this is okay. Reminds me that I can hold sorrow and joy both. That I can be confused and calm in the not-knowing. Wants me to know that being messy is great—messy is human. My wildness is messy.

creativity is not for the purpose of an outcome or product
creativity is to
stir up your passion
free your Spirit and
save your Soul

Chapter 10

Wild Bodies/Moving Our Bodies

> "Your body is the ground metaphor of your life, the expression of your existence. It is your Bible, your encyclopedia, your life story." – Gabrielle Roth

Our bodies are wild. They want to move wildly and move often. When we feel fully alive in our bodies, when we fully accept all of ourselves and every part of our bodies, only then can we live fully. And that is important. I know you would agree with me that we all want to live fully—for our entire lives. This living fully shouldn't disappear as we age or grow older. If anything, we should feel more alive.

We've talked a lot about our wild feminine spirit and being embodied. Moving our bodies, whether you want to call it fitness or not, is a large part of embracing our wild feminine. Our bodies are wild. Not only do they want to move, but they NEED to move. Without movement, we are not healthy. And without movement we never really learn to love our bodies fully because we never really understand them. Therefore, we never feel really at home in our bodies.

When you move your body you learn so much about yourself. You see the uniqueness that is YOU. You see that you are not everybody else. You do not have to look like everybody else. Your body is unique and it is beautiful and has its own unique abilities.

You get in touch with your strength when you move your body. Whether it be yoga, running, spinning, cycling, weightlifting, or just walking and stretching. You begin to trust that you have the stamina, the strength, the resilience to do anything you want.

You feel alive when you are moving. This might be the most wonderful reason to move. When you are moving fast and hard, you first start to feel your entire body heating up. You begin to feel your quads or hamstrings burn. You feel sweat dripping off your body. Your heart pounds and your breath is deep and full—your lungs are screaming for air. You feel everything else just fall away. You are your body. This is true embodiment. And it is so easy to find. Just move.

Moving your body brings an acceptance, as well as love, for yourself. Because you love what your body is capable of doing. It matters not what others think of your body, because you love how it feels to just move. As a life-long runner, I love to tell myself "the pavement doesn't care how old you are." The bike doesn't care how large you are. Your yoga mat doesn't care how crazy you might feel.

When we find fitness for its own sake—and that looks different for everybody—we become proud of our bodies. Once we are used to that delicious feeling of moving, we find it easy to drop into our bodies. And being in our bodies brings out our wildness. It allows our beautiful feminine wildness, our Shakti, to awaken. Moving my body is very sensuous because it is so easy to FEEL. And that sensuousness is found whether I am running a heart-pumping sprint or doing a slow yin practice or erotically moving to music. Doing any movement or exercise that makes us feel strong and powerful is an aphrodisiac. I feel it is a shame for any woman to grow old and never know how physically strong she is. When we are strong and fluid, we feel sexy, a sexy that has nothing to do with societal standards. A sexy that feels at home in our bodies. So my wish is that you get out there and pump iron, run, jump, dance, just move hard and fast enough that you feel your heart beating in your chest, you feel your blood pumping, and you know you are alive!

As I hope you have seen, there are many ways to learn the art of being embodied. Of living from our feminine bodies rather than in our heads. Utilizing all of them encourages us to live richly full and sensuous lives.

If you've not moved in a long time or if you're trying something new, start slow. That beautiful art of being embodied will allow your body to guide you. So listen. My favorite Mary Oliver quote says, "Let the soft animal of your body love what it loves." And your soft animal body loves to move, loves to feel wild and free.

Moving our bodies . . . ahhhh, it just feels so good. Do you know that feeling? All movement is good but some movement is better than others for allowing our wild feminine to play. She loves organic movement, movement that allows us freedom in our bodies, movement that is not strict and choreographed but rather free flowing and spontaneous.

This spontaneous movement comes from listening to and moving as our bodies desire to move. Often, we start with certain moves, like hip circles, and then after a few moments our bodies begin to show us how to move. In other words, we must get out of our heads and move into our bodies. Which is precisely what we want to do in all of the practices. We desire to be embodied. When we are embodied, our wild feminine self is evident. She is guiding. And it feels like we are home.

This coming home to our bodies is important to our movement. Movement should bring us into our bodies. It will make us feel that our bodies are amazing, that they are sensual, that they feel so good when we just move them as they wish to be moved. And that is not always slow and sensual; sometimes it is wild and chaotic! Our movement is sometimes a way to express our emotions, to move them out of our bodies if we need that, especially emotions that are not serving us. Emotions that we need to let go of.

And I like the idea of moving our bodies throughout the day so they don't get too stiff from too much sitting. Gentle, swaying motions that stir up our blood.

I believe that all movement is beautiful for our bodies. And it doesn't have to be called exercise! One of my favorite ways to move my body is by putting on some music that moves me and just dancing around the house, often naked. The music will always vary depending on my mood. But the movement and the music satisfy my spirit as well as my body. And that's exactly what movement should do.

The simplest, easiest way to get moving is to walk. Outside. Because walking in nature soothes our spirits also. Just lace up your shoes and head out the door. Make it brisk and get your heart rate up. Garden to your heart's content—lots of up and down movements in gardening, plus you have your hands in the earth. Ride a bike, walk on the beach, kayak, do yoga. Just move and enjoy it. Notice how good your body feels as it moves. Begin your movement with a positive attitude. I suggest that before you begin any exercise or movement, you take a moment to give your body some verbal appreciation, thanking her for what she's going to do for you. Your wild woman loves to move in all ways. At first you might feel a little stiff, or awkward, but I promise that if you keep it up, your body will feel better than it ever has before.

A sensuous flowing yoga practice is a beautiful way to not only move your body but to embrace your wild feminine. There is something about moving your body in a slow flowing motion with breath that feels very sensual and begins to awaken your wildness. And it doesn't have to be a complete practice and it doesn't have to look like anyone else's practice. It doesn't even have to look like yoga. Remember, it just needs to feel sweet in YOUR body. As you begin this type of practice, think animal moves. Think of your soft animal body and what it wants. Notice how your dog or cat gently stretches and lengthens its body. It is very fluid, not stiff, and not worried about alignment.

A movement embodiment exercise

Roll out your mat and let's try a few moves. Beginning on all fours and moving with your breath, begin to arch your back on your inhale and round your spine on the exhale. Your inhale lifts your chest and tailbone and your exhale rounds your spine, tucking your tailbone and your chin. Think of all of these moves as undulations. Take a few of these undulations of the spine slowly. Do them slowly and always with your breath. Feel free to sigh out exhales through your mouth, if you wish. You want to relax and find freedom in your body with these poses.

From here, walk your hands forward a little more and begin to circle your hips and pelvis. Start with little circles, mostly in the pelvis and, when it feels right, begin to make your circles larger. Reverse direction when you wish. Gradually begin to make your circles even larger, staying with your breath. Then let your moves become very organic—let your body guide you even deeper. Maybe you drop your pelvis to the earth as you roll through the circles; maybe you press your hips back toward your heels; maybe you slowly roll your hips side to side. Allow your body the freedom to just move. Close your eyes, feel your breath, move with your breath. Sigh or make any sounds that your body wants to make. But mostly just feel. Continue moving this way, making it more and more organic—more and more YOU. Maybe you move in an entirely different direction and that is perfect. Do this for as long as it feels sweet.

Then gently roll down onto your back. Draw your knees into your chest, hugging them in close. Rock just a little side to side. Embrace your own body. Then plant your feet on the floor, near your hips, knees bent. Begin to gently rock your pelvis forward and back, making small pelvic tilts. Go slow and feel your pelvis, your low belly, the center of your wildness. From these pelvic tilts, begin to lift your hips all the way off the floor and gently hold for just a moment. Then begin to circle your hips, slowly and rhythmically, feeling your pelvis lift up and then drop down as you make the circle. Move in both directions. Maybe you'd like to begin to make figure eights with your hips. Feel the sensuousness of this move. Feel free to again make it organically yours. What does your body want to do?

After this, if you wish, just extend your legs, taking a sensual full body stretch, slowly. And then, if you have time, just rest for a few moments, feeling your breath, being aware of your body. If it is at the beginning of your day and you wish to get back to activities, slowly roll yourself up to a seated position and come to standing. From this standing posture, take your feet a little wider than your hips and begin to make hip circles. Eventually move in both directions. Large, small, figure eights, whatever appeals to your body. Do it just because it feels good and your body wants to move that way! And enjoy.

One of the joys of practicing movement alone is that you find the freedom to be yourself, to immerse yourself in your body and move and sigh and moan. Not worried about what someone else might think. For some women this is new ground and it's easier to find this freedom all by yourself.

This is my favorite way to connect with my wild feminine energy and to ground myself within my body and to Mother Earth. The movements can take as long as you want or just be for a few minutes if that's all the time you have. But even in just a few moments, especially with your eyes closed, you begin to feel that connection to yourself again. You feel the wildness in your belly and you welcome her again. And from there, you go about whatever else you need to do with that powerful connectedness to your essence, your wildness. It reminds me that I am woman, that I am wild, and that I am powerful. That I am magic. And you are too.

Remember, we are just remembering who we are, who we have been throughout all times. We are not reinventing ourselves. We are not trying to make ourselves better. We are remembering who we are. And that remembering is so sweet and powerful.

Start your day with movement/My practice

Every day should start with movement. Allowing your body to come alive again. Stretching is my favorite movement first thing in the morning. In fact, as soon as I awake, I take several deep breaths into my belly and then I begin to gently stretch. Slowly lengthening my body, twisting, extending, letting my body guide me. I am still lying in my bed and most of the time my eyes are closed. As I slowly move, I feel into my body, noticing how it is after a night's sleep. I also begin a mental list of things I am grateful for, usually beginning with a good night's sleep and gratitude for breath on this new day.

As I gently continue stretching, I welcome my body into this new day and tell her thank you for just being her. For giving me all the pleasures she has given me. As I do this, I slowly rub my hands over my body, caressing different areas as I thank them and welcome them into this day. My body is a sacred place (as is yours) and I treat her as such. I touch my breasts and my yoni because these are the powerful energy centers of my Shakti. It is a loving caress, not a sexual caress. A sexual caress might arise, if my body feels the desire. No rights or wrongs. Just welcoming my body through touch and movement into this new day. Some days this may take two to three minutes, other days maybe ten to fifteen minutes. Again, think spontaneous rather than requirement. Make it feel good and right to you.

That practice is what I do for gentle movement first thing upon awakening. Maybe you'd like to give it a try. I invite you to try it all and then, as I have said so many times, take whatever resonates with you and make it yours. Always evolving, always changing, just always coming back to our bodies and our desires.

Moving throughout our day, even if just for a few moments, is important for staying present in our bodies. Because every time we move in this way, we arrive back in our bodies. We get out of our heads. And we cannot live with our wild feminine nature unless we are in our bodies. Wild feminine is embodiment. It is who we are naturally. And our wild feminine loves to move our bodies.

So take time for movement throughout your day. Sensuous moves that bring you into your wildness. More challenging aerobic or strength moves like running, or spinning, or weightlifting also bring us into our bodies and make us feel powerful. And powerful is sensuous, especially to our wildness. So make movement that you love, movement that you enjoy, a part of your daily life. Dance of any kind is also a delicious way to move your body.

Doesn't have to be choreographed, just move your body. Earlier I mentioned putting on music that speaks to you in that moment and just move, closing your eyes and letting your body lead. Just you and your body. Feel the sensuousness of it. Or if you are feeling sad, dance your sadness or melancholy. Maybe dance your anger or rage, if that is what you need. By doing this and moving in this way, you are listening to your body. You are listening to your spirit. You are being guided by your wildness. Doesn't it feel good?

Chapter 11

Rituals—Daily Simple Ways to Connect with Your Inner Wildness

> "It always pays to dwell slowly on the beautiful things—the more beautiful the more slowly." – Atticus

Ritual. What does that word mean to you? We think of ritual as a ceremony, an observance, maybe performed the same way every time. I like to think of ritual as being anything that we come to with a sacred intention. Meaning we make it matter to us whether it is important to others or not.

Having small rituals throughout our days and weeks brings much significance and meaning to our lives. And most women are looking for more meaning to their lives. A ritual can be something that I would ordinarily do every day anyway, but I come to it with intention and focus. I come to it with mindfulness. So rituals of any kind bring mindfulness into your life. And mindfulness brings us meaning. Rituals are about holding space for ourselves, in the present moment, honoring all our emotions. And if they are not meaningful to you, then they are not really rituals.

I use rituals every day as a way to bring myself into the moment, into sacredness. They are a means to stay connected to my wild feminine spirit.

Rituals can be as simple or as elaborate as you desire. Nothing is right or wrong. The only requirement is that they speak to you, resonate with you, and serve the purpose of bringing you once again into your wild self and into the moment.

I find that when I add ritual, simple ritual, to the things I do daily, it easily fits into my life. No matter the simplicity, I find myself looking forward to it . . . and missing it when I have not made time for it.

As I share some of my rituals with you, listen, take them—if they resonate with you—and then add to or take away so that the rituals are truly yours. If you are just starting a new ritual, it helps to do it the same way for the first few times. As you practice, you will evolve into your own rituals, your own words. In the beginning, use my words if they feel right to you. But it's better to use your words, to speak from your heart, your belly. In my own rituals, I don't always do or say exactly the same thing every day. I flow with my feelings.

Rituals are important to connect us to the sacredness of the mundane, of the everyday. We are holy creatures and all that we do can be made sacred. When we bring presence and an attitude of sacredness and wonder to anything, that mundane activity becomes sacred, special, rich—preparing a meal, conversation with a friend, making the bed, pleasures, making love. Try it and see.

As I mentioned earlier, most of my rituals are simple. This is one that I do daily, and often more than once a day.

Coffee ritual

Coffee is the first thing I reach for (after my glass of water) in the morning—every morning. Maybe yours is tea. I make a ritual of preparing my coffee by being fully present.

First, I light the candles that sit on my kitchen windowsill. The windowsill itself is an altar to my family, lover, and friends containing small items that bring them to mind.

I choose a specific mug for how I feel that morning. (I love to collect coffee mugs, especially ones with words.) I watch and listen to the water as I slowly add it to the brewer. As the coffee brews I anticipate the delightful aroma and when the coffee is ready, I inhale deeply, often with eyes closed. I pour the coffee into my chosen mug and wrap my hands around the warmth of the mug. I bring the cup right under my nose and inhale deeply, feeling its hot steam wet under my nose. What a delicious smell. As I inhale, I whisper to myself, "I inhale all that is and inhale everything that I need, effortlessly." I am facing my window, which looks directly onto my bamboo and my little altar and candle.

As I take my first sip, slowly, savoring, I say to myself, "I am inhaling all of the elements in this liquid—earth, fire, water, air (coffee beans, sun, rain, wind). I am these elements and they are me. Thank you for the people who made these beans and this coffee possible. May this coffee nourish me."

As I slowly sip the first three to four tastes of my coffee, I give thanks for friends, family, lover, and I am thankful for two to three specific things that day regarding the special people in my life.

I end by asking for magic that day—sometimes for a specific action, if I feel I need that—or just that I feel the magic in any way the universe sends it to me. If I am traveling, I may ask for a magical journey, one in which I keep a magical, positive perspective. I then say, "Thank you, *gracias*" and blow out the candles. Blessed be.

It only takes five or so mindful minutes (less or more as I need it). Yet it brings such a sweet beginning to my day, grounding me in sensory feelings and thankfulness, and a special daily reminder of how special ones have touched my life. This can be done with any beverage you drink in the morning.

Another little ritual I do often with coffee or water is to just breathe my intentions into it. Whatever magic I feel I need at that moment, I just breathe it into my drink as if I were softly blowing out a candle. And then I drink the brew blessed with my intention. This is so easy and is one of my favorites.

I often have more cups of coffee throughout my day. Though I don't go through the entire ritual, I always try to make my first sip one of savoring and gratitude. That alone brings me into the present moment. And that is what ritual is all about.

Morning meditation and gentle movement— ritual

This is how I start every day, adjusting the ritual, or practice, as time allows. See how it sounds to you and then give all, or just part of it, a try. We're going to extend the Begin your Day with Movement that I gave you earlier to include a little more ritual and sacredness.

When you first feel yourself awakening from that deep dream sleep, keep your eyes closed and just gently stretch in a full body stretch. This feels languid and luxurious, sweet and slow, like honey moving. Snuggling even deeper into your bed, with eyes still closed, bring your awareness to your breath. If it feels right, begin to deepen your breath—in through your nose and out with a sigh through your mouth, relaxing into your awakening body, gently stretching it, allowing your body and mind to slowly awaken.

Do this for as long as you wish. As I take my sweet full breaths, I visualize any energies I have picked up from the night leaving my body. I often say silently, "I release all energies I have picked up from the night." Then I call back my own energies, which may have scattered during dreams. I visualize my energies returning, through my root chakra and pelvis and moving up my body. Then, just breathing as my body wants to breathe, I begin to list what I am grateful for as I awaken. I usually begin with thanks for my comfy bed and a good night's sleep, and the gift of a new day.

I end with a positive affirmation such as "Welcome to this new day. It is a beautiful one." All of this can take just a few minutes, if that's all you have. But they are intentional moments intent on welcoming your body and spirit into this day.

Still in my bed, I then move my body slowly through a few more very simple stretches just to see how it feels: drawing knees to chest and circling in both directions, a supine twist to each side, drawing knees to chest again as I rub my feet and circle my ankles. I then lift my legs straight up to the sky, circling my ankles. As I bring my legs to my chest, I gently move my head from side to side, rolling into a sitting position. I twist to each side and then a gentle forward fold over my crossed legs, and maybe then a cat/cow or two. If you are not familiar with this yoga pose, take a seated position and on an inhale breath arch your spine and as you exhale round your spine. It is a practice of undulating the spine.

I don't hold any of these positions, just gently move through them. But as always, you do what feels right to your body that morning. All of this can take just a few minutes in the morning, or you can linger as long as you like. The intent is to start your day being present and fully embodied—a fresh you for a fresh new day. Make it pleasurable for yourself.

None of these rituals or meditations should feel like an obligation. You will return again and again if the end result is pleasure and peace. And as you change, your practices and rituals will change with you. So never be afraid to just explore, to be curious.

Morning blessing or devotional

After I have had my "coffee ritual," I always greet my day with a blessing. I will give you my usual "go to" blessing but I often change it slightly (or a lot) depending on how I am feeling that morning. Again, use my words or choose words that resonate with you.

I open my bedroom window so that I look outside into my front yard or I actually step outside on the earth so that

I can feel and see Mother Earth. I like to see all my plants as I greet my morning.

Morning blessing

I am your daughter, Mama Earth and Mama Moon. I am a child of all the elements—earth, water, air, and fire—and I am at home with all of them. I open my heart to this day with gratitude and love and abundance. I open my body to this day with passion and fire and softness and magic. I am one with everything. May I see the magic in my life today and may I be fully present for all of it. Thank you and blessed be.

Another morning blessing

May I open my heart to this day with joy and gratitude
May I open my body to this day with desire and passion and pleasure
May I feel at home in all I do today
May I touch everyone I meet with love and compassion
May I know that I am enough and
May I immerse myself in the ecstasy and magic of being alive in my beautiful feminine body
Blessed Be

I encourage you to write your own, when the time feels right, using your own words or saying it in your own manner.

That makes it visceral. You want the blessing, or prayer, if you prefer, to be felt in your body. Pray to whomever or whatever speaks to you. Blessings shouldn't be just rote words. When they become that, it's time to change your blessing. Feel it in your bones. Welcome yourself, your body and your spirit, into this new day. And be grateful for all that you have in this precious moment.

Bedtime ritual

I always like to make a little mental gratitude list just before I go to sleep—a reflection on my day and letting go of it all. This day has ended. I reflect back, feeling grateful for the simple things, the people I touched and was touched by, and if something didn't go as I had wanted, I try to find the lesson or the good in it and then let it go. This day has passed and a new one is approaching. No need to linger over it. And then I feel relaxed, grateful, and ready for a good night's rest. My last thoughts before I drift off to sleep are grateful, happy ones. Such good preparation for sleep and it helps me to transition easily into a grateful morning as soon as I wake up. I hope it will do the same for you.

Evening blessing

I have come to the end of my day, Mama Moon. It has been a delicious one. I am grateful for having been able to live my values another day. I have done my best to love fiercely and live slowly. I have felt supported by you and Mama Earth. Thank you. May my body and spirit be nourished with a deep sleep and may I wake refreshed and passionate for a new day. Blessed Be.

Another evening blessing

My body, my heart, and my spirit are grateful for another day. As I reflect upon my day, I let go of what I haven't done and am proud of my accomplishments, however small. I was present and mindful and I looked for magic and wonder in my ordinary day. I will have a sweet restorative sleep and wake refreshed and eager for a new day. Thank you and Blessed Be.

Tiny everyday rituals

Sometimes the best way to be more present in every moment is to make tiny rituals out of the ordinary things we do daily, like the coffee ritual I use every morning.

We all desire to be present through every moment of our lives because we know that when we are present to everything we do, our lives are richer and juicier. As Henry Miller said, "Anything that we give our full attention to becomes wondrous and magical." And we know this to be true.

One of the easiest rituals is to just pause and take three deep breaths. Pausing several times throughout our day to just stop and take three deep full breaths is an anchor into the present moment. Nothing else is required.

Here are some natural transitions throughout your day that are good times to pause and breathe:

* Greeting the morning
* Getting in your car for work
* The transition from work to home
* The transition from evening to bedtime

I have already shared with you the small rituals that I do daily. Some of my rituals are very short, only taking minutes. Others are lengthier. But what really matters is what matters to you. What feels right to you. What brings you into mindfulness of your life. All of it.

Anything we do can be a ritual if approached with intention. And that intention must be very personal. So listen to what I do and say and then play with it. Find the rituals that speak to you personally. That make you feel alive and present. That make you feel grateful. That's the important part, not the ritual itself or how it looks.

A daily habit is a good place to begin to find mindfulness (or ritual) because the act itself is already ingrained in our lives. Most of the time there is a good chance that we just do it in rote without really thinking about it at all. And when that happens, we are usually in our heads ruminating about something past or future. So all we are doing is taking our daily habit and making them moments of mindfulness, moments of presence. What could be better?

Daily habits—morning coffee, taking a shower, your yoga practice, movement exercises that you do, washing your face, massaging oil or cream into your body, sitting down to a meal—are opportunities for a tiny ritual or, if you prefer, just a moment of mindfulness.

Just **lighting a candle** is always a mini-ritual. I have candles in every room of my home. I light the two in my kitchen first thing in the morning as I prepare my coffee. Anytime I feel the need to center myself or connect with my spirit, I light a candle. In the evening, I also light candles throughout my home, setting the intention for slowing down and being present for the evening.

After you light your candle, gaze into the flame for a few moments. Maybe mentally list or make a written list of a few things you are grateful for. Or set an intention for how you wish to feel in that moment—joy, peace, calm. This can be a beautiful meditation. Starting your day with intention and coming back to your intentions throughout the day just by lighting a candle. Try it and see how it feels to you.

Showers and baths are excellent times for ritual. Begin with your sense of smell. Choose a soap or shower gel that smells delicious to you, one you can't resist. Or you might want to rub some essential oil on your body and smell the aroma as the warm water touches your skin. Use your senses in the shower. Being in your body and using your senses brings ritual and mindfulness to anything. Feel the water on your skin, bathe yourself slowly, and feel your hands moving across your body. Pause. Notice how good it feels to just let the warm water pour over your body. So relaxing, even if only for a moment. Be in that moment. As you are drying your body, do you have towels that feel good to your skin? Something that feels luxurious? Doesn't have to be expensive. Just a touch that feels good to you. Then what about massaging your body with an oil or cream that is your favorite scent? I love to make my own essential oil blends with either sesame oil or coconut oil to use for self-massage after my shower. You can choose an invigorating one for the morning and a relaxing serene scent after your evening shower. This entire "shower ritual" takes no more time than your usual shower (except maybe for the massaging of oil onto your skin if you're not used to doing that), but you have been mindful and present. You have been in your body. And you will feel pampered, cleansed, and ready to start your day.

I often use my showers to cleanse my energy. In most of my rituals I like to bring in one or two of the elements (water, fire, air, earth). Water is not only fluid but cleansing and clearing. So when I am in the shower, I imagine (visualize) the water gently washing away any energy that I may have picked up through my day or even washing away the energy of the night. This also works to visually wash away any negativity. Using your imagination is creative and it keeps your mind focused on this moment.

Grounding or earthing. We use grounding and centering a lot in yoga. It is a beautiful practice that brings us a steadiness, a calmness, a feeling of stability. When we are grounded, we feel safe and secure. It is a practice or ritual that should be done daily, maybe even several times during the day when you feel the need to come back to the present, to come out of your head and into this moment in time.

The beauty of grounding or earthing is that it can take just a few minutes or you can make it a longer ritual if you wish or have time.

So let's go back to our mornings again for a minute. How do you start your day? Does this sound familiar? Alarm goes off, you punch snooze a couple of times, then finally dash out of bed, maybe quickly look at your phone. Make a quick cup of coffee and run into the shower and out the door. And maybe you've also helped your kids or partner out the door. You are already rushing around and most likely your mind is racing.

Maybe that is not you. Maybe you have already learned the importance of intentional mornings, no matter how short. Either way, a simple practice of grounding starts all of us in a relaxed, calm manner, feeling that we can handle whatever comes along. We are steady rather than frantic.

My favorite way of grounding is to stand with bare feet on the earth, whether it be sand, grass, or dirt. It only takes a moment or two to feel your feet connecting to the earth. Close your eyes for a couple of deep breaths. Feel the earth's energy rising up into your body and allowing any negative energy you may feel move deep into the earth. Just a simple exchange of energy. If you have the time, you could also sit or lie flat on the earth. Just connecting with nature in this way is soothing to your soul and your nervous system. Many mornings, first thing, I step outside my door and put my bare feet on Mother Earth. A delicious way to start the day. I also do this at the end of my day.

If you cannot find some earth to stand on, there are other very simple ways to ground and center yourself. Simply holding a crystal or stone or even a seashell, all of which carry the earth's energy, in your hand. Close your palm over it and take a few breaths. Feel its energy. Essential oils can also be used to ground us. Usually the heavier, darker oils are grounding—oils such as vetiver, patchouli, frankincense, sandalwood, etc. Just smelling these oils or massaging some into your hands or arms will ground and steady you. As you inhale, pause, close your eyes if you can, and take a couple of deep full breaths.

Grounding meditations are another way to bring you back to your center, to your feelings of serenity. You don't even have to sit on the ground. Finding a comfortable seat, close your eyes and take a few deep full breaths. Feel your connection to whatever you are seated on, feel its hardness, and begin to visualize that you are actually seated on the earth. Feel the earth underneath you. Begin to see roots growing from your spine and hips (maybe visualize your root chakra) growing deep into the earth. In your mind's eye, see your roots connecting with the energy of Mother Earth. For a few moments, a few breaths, stay with this connected exchange of energy. Feel yourself growing calmer. Feel your breath moving through you. When you are ready, begin to draw your roots back up into your body. Thank Mother Earth as you begin to move your body gently and open your eyes. This can last for just a few moments or it can be as long as you need or want it to be. Do what makes you feel grounded.

I also use a quick dip in the ocean as a grounding method, utilizing the elements of water as well as earth.

Centering and calling in my muse. The simple ritual of lighting a candle, closing my eyes and taking a deep breath, asking that my writing or painting come from my heart, my belly, centers me and gets me ready to create. I ask my muse or my wild self to let me write with passion. Very simple but it gets me out of my head and into my body. Reminds me that writing is not thought, it is felt and necessary. Allows me to let go of everything else and just be with my creating. Sometimes I have to pause during my creating and bring myself back into the moment, back into my body, because my inner critic has raised her voice. Like everything else we do, creating is a practice.

Movement rituals. Often when I am running I call in the four elements, naming them and thanking them. Water—the sweat running down my body; fire—the heat of my muscles and my passion that fuel my running; earth—with every step I take, I touch the earth and feel her support; air—the air or wind I feel on my skin as I run. I feel a part of each element.

Do you have any **ritual prayers**, or **meditations**, or **mantras** that you use daily? I call them blessings but substitute the word that resonates with you. I have a blessing every morning as I either look out my window or stand barefoot in my yard. Just touching Mother Earth with my feet or any part of my body is a beautiful ritual for me. I also try to end my day with a blessing, usually just before I drop off to sleep. And often that blessing is just being grateful for a few things that happened that day. I believe that gratitude eases us into a restful sleep and sets us up for waking up with gratitude. These are moments of mindfulness. Maybe you prefer to just sit or lie and focus on your breath . . . taking deep full relaxing breaths.

My blessings themselves change frequently, depending on how I feel. Remember your practice is always evolving, because you are evolving and changing. But when we use words that come from US, that resonate with us, the blessings are so meaningful. And meaningful is what we want. And your blessings may change a little every day. Mine do. I say what I need to say that day. The main thing is that you want to say the words with true meaning and feeling in your heart and your body. You want to FEEL them. They should not just be words that you say without even thinking about them, which sometimes happens if we say the same words over and over. Speak them with feeling.

As you sit down to any meal, take a moment to take a deep breath and be grateful for the food you are about to eat, for the elements of earth, fire (sun), water, and air that are in your food, as well as all the people responsible for bringing this food to you. Only takes a moment, but with this moment, you have brought intention to your meal. Whatever we bless and are grateful for nourishes our body and spirit.

I also like to have a small transitioning ritual as I move from one task to the next. In my case it is often moving from one class to the next or from client to client. Maybe your transitions are when you start a new project. Or we all have the transition from work to home or day to evening. This small little ritual is just a way to bring mindfulness to these transitions. Making them important. As you begin to make the transition, pause for a moment and take a deep breath or two. You don't have to sit, you don't have to close your eyes. You might want to set an intention for whatever you are moving toward next, whether it be a project, a client, or time with family and loved ones. An intention is a desire for how you wish to feel. While a goal is focused on the future, an intention is focused on the present moment. Who you are in this present moment. An example of an intention might be, "I want to feel as much joy as possible as I tackle this next project." Or "I intend to be fully present when I am with my loved one."

Word of the day, word of the month, and/or word of the year is also an amazing little ritual to bring intention to your day. I love to choose a word of the year. This intention will guide me throughout the year, reminding me to make decisions and take action based on my intention for the year. In past years my words have been pleasure, peace, adventure, desire, yes, serenity. This year my word is juicy. When I choose to do something, think something, feel something, I ask myself, "Is this going to make me feel juicy in my body, mind, or spirit?' See how that works. I have used this for several years and have found it to work perfectly for me. Of course, sometimes you may want or need to change your word as you move through the year. That is perfect. Remember you are evolving.

I often choose a word for the day also. This is setting an intention for the day of how I wish to feel, how I wish to act. Giving that feeling just one word makes it so easy to come back to my intention throughout the day. It gives me focus. And if you are a word person like me, you will love this little ritual.

What words speak to you? As I choose my word for the year, I let it simmer in my body and on my mind for days, maybe trying one out to see how it feels in my body. You will know when the "right" word appears, trust me. Then you can come up with ways to take that word with you. I usually have a necklace or bracelet made with my word. I often write my word in my journals, on my mirrors, etc.

Sometimes I write my word on a small stone or crystal, something small that I can use as a touchstone. A touchstone is something you carry with you that holds the intention of your word so that just by touching it you are reminded of your desire. Play with it. What calls you?

I invite you to make a list of some of your daily habits and then choose two or three that you'd like to bring ritual or intention to. There are so many times throughout the day that we can ritualize. Don't make it too lengthy or difficult. Just think of the intention you would like to bring to that moment. Remember, you're just holding space for yourself. Be playful. Though it is a spiritual sacred practice (for me), that doesn't mean you have to be overly serious. Enjoy it. These moments, these rituals, should make you feel good. Should add to your day. Should bring you pleasure.

If it doesn't bring you joy, doesn't make you happy, why do it?

Essential oils

Essential oils are another way I create ritual and one way I move into my body every day. And the oils are also my medicine cabinet and cleaning supplies. This comes from my love of my body and my love for Mama Earth and the universe.

I love to make my own massage oils for my body, face oils, scrubs for exfoliating, and "concoctions" for my health and hygiene. If you've never done it, I highly recommend buying a few essential oils and playing with them.

An essential oil is the soul of the plant or flower. When we use essential oils, we are taking the essence or soul of that plant into our bodies, for healing, for pampering. Essential oils affect us physically as well as emotionally. And the act of making my lotions and "potions" feels a little bit like magic to me. I often choose my scents by their properties—not just physical properties, but their emotional properties. In other words, I make my blends with intention—maybe an intention to heal, or an intention to soften and make juicy, or a lotion to help me sleep. And I know as I make these that everything I put into and on my body is pure. I have made it myself with a carrier oil, such as coconut oil or sweet almond oil, to which I have added a few essential oils of my choice. And my body and mind is absorbing all that goodness. When putting essential oils on your body, always dilute with a carrier oil.

I also make blends that I diffuse through my house. These blends affect the energy of my home and the people in it. I use blends for purifying, cleansing, adding a little intimacy, and sometimes just to give my home a wonderful peaceful aroma. Many of my blends are for grounding, mostly because I almost always feel the need to ground and center and I just adore the rich earthy scents of essential oils that are grounding.

Chapter 12

The Moon and Moon Cycles

"As if you were on fire from within, the moon lives in the lining of your skin."
- Pablo Neruda

The moon is so closely connected to our wild divine feminine. Just as much as Mama Earth. The moon's energy is feminine and she shows us our own cycles of feminine energy—periods to renew, times to grow and do, times to let go. The moon has a pull on our energies and our bodies and draws us to her every night. Showing us that we are creatures of wildness, of wholeness, that we contain all the emotions, that we are emotional creatures. She asks us to embrace our wildness, our cycles of living. Plus, she is just so beautiful that how could you not want to connect with her.

For several years I have tuned in to the cycles of the moon using them as my calendar—for planning, for intention setting, for letting go, for creating rituals during each cycle. I have found it to be one of the best ways to keep inviting in my wild feminine, to stay in touch with my sense of wholeness, wildness, and feminine power. The moon gives me two opportunities every month—new moon and full moon—to reframe, rethink, set new intentions, or give up something. With the cycles of the moon, I am always coming back to myself, being asked to go within and listen. Connecting to the moon connects us to our intuition, our deepest knowing. For the moon is intuitive and she teaches us how to listen to that part of ourselves. Connecting with the moon teaches us to trust our own knowing and, maybe more importantly, to trust in our not-knowing. Because even in our not-knowing we know, maybe not consciously, but we KNOW deep inside our bodies. And we also trust deep inside our bodies. Trust that our paths are still there. They just aren't visible to us at the moment. The moon, just like the earth, helps us build our resilience by showing us that there will always be ebbs and flows. And ebbs and flows are exactly how life is lived. There is no control. Just trust in the ebb and flow of life, of our emotions and feelings, of the events in our lives.

Creating rituals around the cycles of the moon brings sacredness into our lives and strengthens our connection to the natural cycles of the world—the sacredness of the universe. I create rituals for the dark moon, the new moon, and the full moon. Remember that your rituals need to feel purposeful to you. They should incite a little passion and purpose into YOUR life, no one else's.

The dark moon is the time just before the new moon. There is no moon visible. This is a time for rest and deep introspection. Looking inward to see what we have been letting go of as the moon was waning and to fully surrender anything that is still lingering. Seeing how far we have come.

The new moon is usually seen as a magical time to set intentions and manifest. Because over the next two weeks, as the moon grows to full, is a time of waxing, growing. And the seeds that we plant, our intentions and desires, use this waxing energy of the moon to grow and expand into our desires. The waxing moon is a time for action.

New moon ritual example

Light a candle of your choice. I often use a black candle for the new moon. Play some music that either soothes or arouses you. Let it elicit a feeling. Sit comfortably and take a few deep breaths, settling into your body. I sometimes journal as I am thinking about my intentions. Your intentions will be your strongest desires for the coming weeks. In order to manifest our intentions, we must have a strong visceral feeling in our bodies, a strong desire. Write your intentions in a positive way, such as "I desire to have a passionate, loving relationship." Feel your intention in your body and expand upon it as much as you wish. Feel as if you had that relationship already. Once you've set your intentions, it is time to converse with Mama Moon. I always like to do this sitting outside under the night sky. The new moon is often not visible at this time, but her energy is there. I speak to her about my deepest desires. I always feel it is best to just use your own words. They are more meaningful to you and that is what is important. When finished, thank Mama Moon. End your ritual with a few deep breaths. You may put your intentions in your journal or in a sacred place on your altar or, if you prefer, some place where you can see them daily. Revisit your intentions as the moon waxes. This is the time to take intentional action toward your desires.

The full moon is an excellent time to look back at the intentions you set during new moon and see what has come to light. Is it an intention that has been growing? Is it still an intention that you wish or does it want to be tweaked a little? We use the illumination of the full moon's light to shine upon our lives and our actions.

Under this illumination, we may find things that we want or need to let go of. The full moon is an excellent time for letting go as the moon's energy will now begin waning, eventually fully letting go back to the dark moon and then another new moon. The full moon also illuminates all we have to be grateful for. The full moon's energy is powerful so use this energy for whatever you most desire.

Full moon ritual example

Remember, your rituals can be as simple or as elaborate as you like. Sit comfortably on the ground. During the full moon, I like to do my entire ritual outside under the glow of the moon, weather permitting. Light a candle. I usually use a white candle, symbolizing the illumination of the full moon. In this ritual I begin with gratitude. Talking to Mama Moon with my own words, thanking her for all the abundance I have had since the past full moon. Then I review the intentions I set at the new moon, seeing how far I've come and if I feel the need to add to them in any way. Once again, asking for the energy of the moon to manifest my desires. Then I look at what I may need to let go of as this moon wanes. Most of the time it is just feelings or an old way of life that I need to release. And sometimes I have to keep letting go of something for a while before I truly feel I have left it behind. I write these down on paper. Then, to signify that I am ridding myself of these, I either burn them in a fireproof dish or I tear them up and throw them away. If I burn my list, I bury the ashes in the earth. Remember that the full moon is powerful and easily illuminates our gratitudes, manifests our desires, and encourages us to let go and surrender. As I talk with Mama Moon, I have a glass of wine. And during the full moon, I often moonbathe naked under her beautiful energy, allowing her energy to flow into me. There is nothing much better than lying on the earth, naked, under the full moon. Please try it when you can in some secluded place. You will be able to feel the energies of the earth as well as the moon.

All of these moon cycles are excellent times to journal. Pick up your pen and write your feelings and emotions at each cycle. Write what you are letting go of and write your greatest desires, your intentions for the next cycle. Write your gratitude.

Just these simple rituals and ways of looking at the moon's cycles keep us connected to the universal truths and energies, keep us engaged with the earth and the moon. And the moon allows us to closely examine our desires, our lives, every two weeks. From these reflections, we then create action steps when deemed necessary. We also learn from the moon cycles that there are times when we are waiting, waiting for answers, waiting for the perfect time to move forward. Using those times to nourish ourselves.

Connecting with the moon and her cycles draws us deep into our wild feminine energy. The goddess energy is in the moon. The moon is everything feminine. If we sit quietly, we can feel her pull.

Have you ever been drawn to the moon and weren't exactly sure why? You just know that you need to go outside, look up in the dark sky, and see the moon in all her beauty. You feel that pull. That is your divine wild feminine calling. Honor her. Spend time outside under the moon. Lie on the earth under the moon. Moonbathe whenever you can. Nude, if possible. Soak in the energies of the moon in all her magnificent power. For her power is your power. Her magic is your magic.

Chapter 13

Pleasure and Desire

"Every desire of your body is holy."
– Rumi

What brings you pleasure? Do you really know what makes you feel amazing and brings a huge smile to your face? Knowing what brings us pleasure and happiness gives us permission to bring more of that into our lives. Running and sex with someone I love are my two favorite ways to feel pleasure. Though these always work for me, there are times when I desire pleasure and joy and I just don't have time for either of those. So in those times, I have many different choices of joy-bringing "things" that I can turn to. Maybe I'll read something inspiring on my phone or watch a short funny video, or maybe I'll brew a cup of coffee and just smelling that delicious aroma begins to fill me with joy, or I'll just stop and take four or five breaths deep into my belly and list a few things that I cherish. That one always works. All sorts of things can bring us pleasure and the list will vary by person. But it is crucial that we know what makes us feel wonderful and maybe stimulates desire—just so we can have more of that.

If you've not already done so, I invite you to begin making a list of things that bring you pleasure. All sorts of things, large and small, some that take a long time, others that only require a few minutes. Then begin to choose from your lists. Do something, at least one thing, that brings you pleasure every day. Soon, you'll be doing things all day long that bring you pleasure. Because you are focusing on pleasure. You are focusing on yourself. It will be your intention to find pleasure, joy, and happiness. And that makes for a beautiful day and a joyful life.

Desire

What a beautiful word "desire" is. Desire is the strong feeling of wanting something. We often use the word craving to express desire. What other words do you use to describe your desire? What kinds of feelings does the word "desire" stir in your body?

Desire is the essence of our wild divine feminine. Yearning is our true nature. This is how we create anything and everything. What are your feelings toward your desires? Your longings?

I believe desire and longing have been given a negative bias, especially for women. Because of this, we often don't feel comfortable with our desires. Maybe we downplay them as not really being necessary. Or maybe we're ashamed of them or don't believe we deserve what we yearn for. The most tragic is that some have even lost touch with what they desire. They've pushed their desires away for so long that now they don't even recognize them.

Desire—yearning—is crucial for a rich, meaningful, yes, juicy, life. Without desire, there is no joy, no pleasure. There is no moving toward, or opening up, to receive the lives we are meant for. Desire gives our lives meaning. So what have you desired lately? Is there something, or someone, you are currently yearning for? Are you open to your desire? How does desire feel in your body?

Without desire, there is no creating. We create because we have a desire for something, a yearning for something. It doesn't mean we're not living in the present. We are. We are not just idly wishing for something in the future. I'm talking about those deep desires we feel in our belly, in our bodies, those yearnings that call us forth to be more present, more immersed in life. True desire can only be felt in the present.

Of course, we also have those sweet little desires for chocolate, dancing in the rain, wine. And though those may sound simple, they can also be life-changing in their own way. And if we've been out of touch with our desires, small ones are just the place to begin.

How does desire "feel" to you? Just sit for a moment and listen, feel. Just by doing that, you are using embodiment. You are noticing how something feels in your body—in this instance how a word resonates within you. This can powerfully tell us how we feel about things, how we view our world, and even what limiting beliefs we may have.

So how did you feel? Desire is one of my favorite words. Just the sound of it brings such delicious feelings to my body. We can desire so many things, no right or wrong, but in order to feel desire, we must feel in our bodies that desire is a beautiful, necessary thing. Just as we talked about the necessity of sensuality, desire goes hand in hand with sensuality and embodiment. When was the last time you felt desire, even just a little? Were you aware of it, and did you embrace it and let it move through your body? Desire can be as simple as my desire for my first cup of coffee every morning. I feel it in my body and when I take that first slow sip, I am rewarded with a feeling of deliciousness—having received what I wanted—and I savor those sips.

Desire brings us into the present moment if we allow it. Allowing ourselves to feel the desire right now, even though it may not be satisfied in the present moment. And, as with so many other things, desire is about the want, the need, more than about having the desire satisfied, though, of course, that feels amazing also. But we want to allow ourselves to feel the desire. Nothing is ever created without desire. Desire stimulates us to create, to move toward our desires, to dream. Desire is a rich emotion that brings us a love of life. Desire creates abundance in our lives.

Like many other emotions, we often don't give ourselves permission to feel too much desire. Because we are afraid of it. Where might it lead? So first, we may need to just trust that desire is necessary for a sweet life. Whether it is desire for something or someone or possibly a desire for a feeling and state of being. All are good and worthy and you are worthy of these sweet feelings.

So take a few moments to sit and answer a few questions. It is better to write than just think about your answers. There is a clarification and a "knowing" that comes from expressing our words and thoughts on paper. So give it a try.

Journaling prompts

- ✶ What does desire mean to me?
- ✶ Where in the past few days/months have I felt desire? For what, whom?
- ✶ How did this desire make me feel?
- ✶ How much desire do I allow myself to feel?
- ✶ What fears do I have around desire?

As you write, notice feelings in your body—any softening, or gripping. Just paying attention.

Now that you've looked at your feelings around desire, let's see if you can bring more desire into your life.

Remember always, just baby steps if this is new for you. If you are really good at this already, have fun adding a few more desires to your week. See if you feel more alive.

Make a list of small things you desire. Things that are pretty easy to satisfy at some point. Maybe list five to ten things. Looking over your list, choose one that you want to focus on now. Sit with that idea for a moment, taking a few deep breaths. See if just by thinking about it and feeling it in your body, you can begin to feel your desire grow. Go ahead, just breathe into it and let it grow. Now go about whatever you are doing, and keep coming back every now and then to your feeling of desire, of want. Then begin to plan when you will satisfy that desire, sometime when you have the time to really savor it. Make sure you chose something that is fairly easy to satisfy.

Throughout the week, keep coming back to your list of desires and activate another one or two. You may even find that you have come up with new and more desires. Give yourself permission to just enjoy your desires.

Remember that our wild feminine nature IS DESIRE. Just as she IS sensuality, creativity, sexuality, passion, compassion, rage, sorrow. All of these beautiful, raw, human emotions are embodied in our wild feminine nature. And as we embrace this creature that is us and has been us all along, we understand that all of our rawness, our emotions, are the essence of who we are. We want them, we want to share them, we love them and embrace them. Because they bring us back to our wildness, to our authenticity, to our essence.

Your mantra: "I fiercely and fearlessly love myself in all my messiness and rawness and beauty. I am a creature of desire and sensuality. I am a creature of desire and sensuality."

Repeat it, repeat it, repeat it until you believe every word. And you will. I promise.

Pleasure

Do you know what turns you on in life? What brings you great pleasure, what brings you fully into the present moment? Because that's what pleasure does. It brings us into this moment. We become focused on our sensations. Everything else just drifts away.

But often we've lost touch with what turns us on, with what stirs our passion. That's a sad place to be. Life feels meaningless, or at best, boring. Nothing excites us.

What makes you want to get up in the morning, excited to start your day? What stokes your fires?

Let's see if we can take your smoldering embers and create a raging fire, one that will consume you in its warmth and passion. We'll start slowly.

Maybe start with your list of small things you have been doing for yourself. If you allow yourself to fully immerse yourself in them, even these small things feel delicious. Pleasure and passion are that way. We won't really feel either unless we lose ourselves in that moment, in whatever we're doing, whether it's making love, or painting, or just savoring a meal. If we don't lose ourselves in it, we cannot experience it fully, passionately, richly. And isn't this how we want to experience everything? Continue to explore letting go of control and losing yourself in the moment, whatever that moment is.

Your wild feminine desires to feel life in this way. This is what makes her (you) alive.

Remember some moments in your life when you've been filled with passion, so much so you feel it dripping out your pores. You feel juicy, decadent, alive.

Feel those moments fully right now. How do they taste? Can you smell them? Bring them to you fully. What are you doing? Are you with someone or by yourself?

Our wild self is full of passion. We don't have to have someone to feel it with, though we can also share exquisite passion purely because we know how to feel it. We have been there many times. Passion can be shared but it is also a solitary experience. Both are valuable. I have seen far too many women give up on passion because there is no one in their lives at the moment. This is sad. Passion can and should be explored by yourself. Passion is life and life is passion. It is that simple. And once you KNOW passion, it is easy to share your passion if you wish.

What is one small pleasure you can give yourself now? Ignite your fires slowly, but I promise you they'll grow quickly. Your body yearns for pleasure and passion. So give it a try, maybe giving yourself permission to savor a decadent piece of chocolate, maybe several pieces.

Stoking our fires is not the time for restraint. Just taste with feeling. Inhale the chocolate before you place it in your mouth. Then put a small piece in your mouth. Feel the heat of your mouth melt it slowly, the sweetness moving over your tongue and teeth. Don't swallow it yet. Close your eyes. As you swallow slowly, taste that first taste and see if you can taste it all the way down. Pause. Savor. How is the sweetness lingering in your mouth? Ahhh . . .

Now try this with something else. Immerse yourself in whatever you wish. Don't hold yourself back. Most of us are better at restraints than we are at letting go fully and immersing into anything. Most of us want to hold back just a little. So taste, move, feel with abandon. Be free. No restraints.

Nourish your body with pleasure and sensuality. Nourishing your body is not an obligation or should not be seen as something or some way to "get into shape."

By embracing your sensuality, by owning it, by cherishing your deep inner feminine energy, your Shakti, you will bring passion, joy, creativity, richness into your life. You will be in love with your life. You will find ease within your life.

Loving who you are frees you up to be authentic . . . in all your loveliness and messiness, your chaos and calm. All of it is you. Trust your passion, trust your emotions, live from your feminine essence—no apologies. Be guided by the deep intuition of your belly.

You are complex and complicated. Have no fear of pleasure, sensuality, or desire. You are made for these.

Our wild self is intimate with pleasure in all its forms. She knows that she is made for pleasure. Pleasure, even the simplest, is only felt and sensed in the moment, one of the reasons it is so powerful.

As modern women, it is sometimes hard for us to feel pleasure. We've been in our heads too long and have forgotten how it feels. We cannot truly feel pleasure unless we are connected to our bodies. While in our heads, pleasure cannot be felt as deeply because we are not attuned to our bodies' sensations, which is where pleasure is felt.

Pleasure, whether sensual or sexual, needs relaxation, softness, and receptivity. When we're always in "do" mode or constantly feeling anxious or stressed, it is extremely difficult to feel pleasure or to even want to feel just the anticipation of pleasure.

Yet there are many reasons why so many feel a disconnect to their bodies and/or always being in their heads. Our culture is one that honors and praises being in our heads. Thinking is a much greater quality than is feeling. Therefore, many of us spend so much time in our heads, and have for so many years, that it feels as if it is the only place we live. It's as if we forget that we even have bodies. They are little more than an inconvenience. How sad this is. Because we are our bodies.

As we are growing up and even now as adults, society and the media are inundating us with messages of how our bodies should look, what parts are "bad," what is wrong with us, that we are too old. Most of the time we begin to believe this and we learn to hate and shame our bodies because they are not what they should be. We sometimes begin, even at a very young age, to disconnect from our bodies. Until, finally, we are not sure we can even find and come back to our bodies. They just don't feel familiar.

And most certainly, as we were beginning to explore our bodies, we were never told, "Yes, that is great. Explore your body and find out how it brings you pleasure." How would it feel to grow up in a culture like that? Instead, most of us were told, "Don't touch yourself, that's nasty." So many of us grow up thinking it is wrong to be in our bodies, wrong to touch ourselves, and wrong to feel pleasure.

But you can change that train of thought, that perspective, by giving yourself permission to re-connect with your body and to explore pleasure in all its forms. And know that it is okay to do so. And I hope I have given you enough reasons so far that you WANT to reconnect and explore. You desire it. That's the best start.

Journaling prompts

Make a list of things that bring you pleasure, things that turn you on.

We cannot feel the full spectrum of pleasure if we don't learn to relax. Getting out of our heads and into our bodies is required. And if we struggle with the idea of all this being wrong or just not right, then we definitely have to relax into our bodies first. And breath is the way to do that.

Just as we use our breath as a tool in yoga and meditation, breath is also used in Tantra and Tantric sexual practices. Our breath is such a beautiful tool because it is always with us, readily accessible. And our breath is one of our automatic bodily functions that we can control to some extent. Becoming aware of our breath enables us to move into our bodies, just by feeling the breath. And as we focus on our breath and begin to drop out of our heads into our bodies, we begin to move into that part of our nervous system that relaxes and heals, our parasympathetic nervous system. As we continue to feel our breath, our breathing becomes deeper and slower and we begin to feel more relaxed, we begin to feel a softness in our minds as well—thoughts lessening and becoming quieter. We begin to find that essence of calm that is always with us.

As we find this beautiful softening of our bodies, we are more primed to feel pleasure, any kind of pleasure. This is a great place to start as you begin to practice the body meditations and touching I have given you (in previous chapters). Starting from this relaxed place, your mind is less likely to interfere with those old limiting beliefs.

Now let's take this softening of our bodies specifically into our lower bodies. The abdominals, pelvic floor, and hips of many women are in a constant state of gripping. This comes from sitting at computers, feeling anxious and/or stressed. There is a tightness that never lets go. And a constricted body cannot feel pleasure. In fact, often all we feel is numb. Sensation can't go through.

Through some fluid movement practices, we will begin to loosen that gripping. We want and need our lower bodies to be responsive and receptive. Life will feel freer, our bodies will feel freer.

For many woman, the only sensations they can feel are dramatic, large sensations—jolts, cold, harsh touch.

As we begin to "free" our lower bodies, we will also teach ourselves to feel and appreciate the tiniest of sensations. And from there we can begin to anticipate pleasure throughout our day—and through many different sensations. Pleasure is felt in all our senses.

Sensual embodied movement practice for your hips and pelvis

We will begin with some gentle pelvic tilts. Put on comfortable clothes or, if it feels right, do this nude. Most of you are familiar with pelvic tilts, but we're going to concentrate on the subtlety of the movement.

Lie flat on your back on your yoga mat or bed. With bent knees, place your feet hip width apart. Take a few deep breaths into your belly, relaxing your body into the earth (surface) beneath you. Place your hands on your lower belly. On your exhale breath, very gently tilt your pubic bone toward your belly button, an almost imperceptible move, but you should feel your lower back flatten.

As you inhale, softly release your pubic bone toward the mat. You will feel your low back lift up slightly. As you inhale, make a conscious effort to relax your pelvic floor. Begin by softening your belly, your glutes (bottom), and your thighs. When you are using your pelvic floor (on your exhale as above), you feel a pulling or engagement in your yoni and rectum. When you relax your pelvic floor muscles, you feel a softness in your yoni and rectum. In the beginning you may not feel any sensation in your pelvic floor, but just keep visualizing until you do.

Repeat these moves several times with your eyes closed, allowing yourself to drop deeper into your body with every breath. See if you can begin to receive sensations from these small movements of your pelvis. What do you feel? Just be curious. And if you don't feel anything, that's okay too. Just keep relaxing into it. The more you relax, the more you feel. It just takes time.

After several breaths with your pelvic tilts, make your way to all fours. Still on your bed is fine. Widen your knees a little and take a deep inhale into your belly and a long sigh out through your mouth. Allow your body to soften into this pose. Think of the element of water. This is your feminine element. Drop into your belly, your pelvis. With eyes closed, begin to gently move your body. There is no right or wrong way. Maybe you begin to sway your hips side to side or circle your hips and pelvis.

From these gentle, fluid movements, let your body take you where it wants to go. Just breathe deeply, making your exhales a little longer than your inhales. And I encourage you to sigh, if that feels right. Sigh loudly. Bring the emotion out of your body and into a sigh or a moan. Just keep your eyes closed and move.

Maybe you drop your pelvis forward as your head relaxes and rolls side to side. Use your breath to let go of any gripping, especially in your pelvis. See if you can feel as if you're breathing space into your pelvis, your yoni. Keep your awareness there. Expand. Move freely. And if it feels weird at first, don't worry. You will eventually begin to feel freer, I promise.

Move like water, making sounds as you wish, for a few minutes, or as long as it feels sweet. Then slowly bring your body to stillness. Come to table pose on all fours. Your hands are directly under your shoulders and your knees are under your hips. Your spine is long. In this pose, you actually resemble a table. From table pose, take your knees wide and then slide your hips back to your heels. If your hips don't come all the way down to your heels comfortably, lower them as far as you can. This is called Child's Pose in yoga. You want this to be a relaxing pose. Find your comfortable place and breathe slowly and deeply.

Both of these movements will begin to open your pelvic area and your hips. Best of all, they will help you begin to truly feel this area, allowing you to soften and release.

Embracing your wild feminine is being deeply in touch with your lower belly, your pelvis, your yoni. This is where your feminine power is, your wisdom, your guidance. This is your intuitive nature.

Often we find ourselves not very connected to our "feminine parts," sometimes just from busyness and neglect, sometimes from shame or trauma. But you are going to love this part of yourself, even adore this part of you, your true feminine essence, as you live from your ancient wildness.

You will begin to trust "her" and, most importantly, honor her as the sensual, powerful, loving creature she is. She is you and you are her.

So I invite you to practice these two easy movements often. Maybe daily. See how your practice, your movements, change. Notice emotions arising. How do you feel after? I invite you to do this regularly, even if you're saying right now, "I'm already in touch with my sensuality, my womanly parts." This will only expand your depth of feeling, of trust.

Later, we will go even deeper into our sensuality, but for now, enjoy these often.

Chapter 14

Sensuality

"Passion gives me moments of wholeness." – Anais Nin

So here we are at my favorite part! And I hope it will be yours also—if not this moment, very soon in the future. Because through sensuality and sexuality, we truly embrace our wild feminine self. Without sensuality and/or sexuality, that Shakti fire, we are not truly living in our beautiful wildness, our authenticity as a woman.

Does even the thought of embracing and honoring your sexuality scare the hell out of you? Or do you find it a little intriguing? Or are you grinning and saying, yes, let's do this? Any or all are just perfect. So no judging. We always start right where we are, remember? Always! And it is important to know where you are beginning, where you are right now.

Before we get into that, let's talk a little about how sensuality and sexuality are such a delicious part of our wild feminine. As women, we are sensual creatures. We may have lost that along the way but our true nature is sensual. Sensual means that we live and use our bodies through our sense of touch, taste, smell, feeling, hearing, etc. One of the reasons sensuality is so vital is that we cannot be fully embodied without being immersed in our senses, and when we are immersed in our senses we are being sensual. It is as simple as that. Sensuality is not complicated and it is not always, by any means, related to sexuality. Sensuality is, in and of itself, a magical way to live our lives.

So how do you feel about your own sensuality? Is it something that you own and practice? Do you notice when you feel sensual? Do you know what things make you feel that way? This is what you will be doing at first—just exploring. Being curious about the touch, taste, and feel of things that just make you feel good. That make you feel delicious. Sensuality makes us feel alive and whole and juicy.

Our wild feminine thrives on sensuality. It is her nature. If you are feeling disconnected from yourself, there is a great chance that you have not been giving yourself enough sensual playtime throughout your days and weeks. Remember, we are just talking about things that make you feel sweet, that bring a little delicious touch to your days.

Sensuality is a one-person activity. You need no one else to imbibe in your sensuality. Being aware of every smell, sound, touch, and sight begins your journey to sensuality. Notice how the raindrops lightly caress your skin, how the colors of the sunset wrap the world in beautiful light, how juicy mangoes literally drip over your lips and fingers. Pay attention to the world and how it affects YOU, how it makes you feel.

Think of eating and savoring a sweet little dessert—chocolate, anyone? Or snuggling up in a warm fuzzy blanket, reading a tantalizing book, choosing to wear clothes that feel deliciously soft on your skin and make you smile, massaging and anointing your body with your favorite essential oils. See, it is easy and not very time consuming. But we have to be mindful of it, especially in the beginning. Searching and finding things that feel good to us, things that make us feel juicy, and then taking the time to do them, taste them, smell them, touch them.

The most difficult part for many women is just allowing themselves to feel sensual. Giving themselves permission to open their bodies and hearts to sweet sensuality in all its forms. We're afraid to eat that piece of cake. Oh God, where might it lead? We're afraid to massage our bodies with essential oils because we haven't touched our bodies in such a way in a long time—with mindful, loving touch. We are afraid of too much pleasure, even the simple kinds. When we open ourselves to such pleasures, we soon see how much joy and ease and grace they bring us. Life itself becomes sweeter. We are happier.

So let's begin your exploration of where you are. Maybe sit with the questions below. Find a quiet spot where you have a few minutes to yourself. Begin by taking a few deep breaths into your belly. As you sit with the questions, just notice what arises in your body. Do you feel tightness or tension? Or, as you begin to ponder the questions, do you feel a lightness, an openness? Remember that all is perfect. I encourage you to write your answers after a few moments. Just put your feelings down on paper without editing them. Let your heart and body write. And you may want to do this a few times.

Journaling prompts

- What does the word "sensuality" mean to me? What does it bring to mind? How does it feel in my body, especially in my belly?
- Which of my senses do I use the most? Which brings me the most pleasure? Do I prefer soft touch, amazing smells, etc.?
- Can I think of myself as sensual without thinking of sex?
- If I am feeling sensual, how do I feel? And if I can't remember, how do I imagine I would feel?
- When you feel ready, make a list of sensual activities that you might like to do. They can be the tiniest

things. Don't make a big production out of it. But by all means, if there is something you REALLY want to do, go for it! Enjoy yourself. You can edit the list later. This should be fun and, hopefully, make you feel a little desirous.

Because that's what sensuality does. Makes us feel desirous. Those sweet pleasures in life bring us joy, make us feel alive. Your wild feminine epitomizes desire. The journey to sensuality and desire is a delicious one indeed.

So have you come up with your list yet? I'll give you a few ideas if you need them. Take them and then add on, making your list specifically desiring to YOU.

- Sipping a cup of hot chocolate, or maybe a glass of wine
- Watching the sun rise over the ocean
- A few soft throws on your bed or soft new sheets
- Making yourself a delicious meal of only those foods you love
- Watching the full moon rise over the ocean
- Standing in a gentle rain and letting it wash over you, feeling every raindrop
- Diffusing a scent through your house that smells delightful to you
- After your shower, slowly massaging a warm oil into your skin

Is that a good start for you? What comes to mind as you think about ways to make yourself feel good? What do you enjoy looking at? What can you bring into your house that makes you smile just to look at it?

Sensuality will make you smile, it will bring a warmth to your body, it will make you feel ripe and juicy. All sensual practices should be something that brings you joy. And in taking time for even those few small minutes of joy, we bring such richness to our lives.

Bringing sensuality back into our lives reinforces the belief that we are worthy. We are worthy of beauty that makes us smile, of touch that makes us feel good. Just as with gratitude, the more we practice sensuality, the more we desire it and the easier it becomes to find ways to bring more sensuality into our lives.

Your homework for now is to look at your list and choose two or three items that you will do in the next week. Just for yourself. They can be small things but, if possible, try to have one that takes a little more time and then make the time for it, make the time for yourself. Remember, you are worth it. This is not frivolous. This is a necessity. And as you begin to practice feeling sensual, you will soon realize how necessary it is. And how sweet it makes you feel. You will also find a whole new way of seeing yourself.

Sensuality is a beautiful way to begin to really practice self-love. To know your worth. To show yourself love and desire. And we cannot share that love and desire with someone else until we feel it for ourselves.

So stop reading and go do something sensual! Or maybe two things if you are feeling adventurous! And maybe write down how you felt. Eventually, let your entire day be led by sensuality.

One of my mantras for this year has been "If it doesn't bring me joy, juiciness, or an orgasm, I won't do it!" How about you?

A journaling practice for sensuality

- Write five things that you can see right now
- Write five things you can hear right now
- Write three things you can touch right now
- Write one thing you can taste right now

If you wish, you can begin with "Here, right now, in this moment, I touch . . ." then include whatever is meaningful to you, e.g., the lusciously soft blanket covering my lap, the silky belly fur of Gracie, the crisp hardness of a green apple with my mouth.

Chapter 15

Sexuality and Pleasure

> "Oh Radiant One, ride the waves of ecstatic motion into a sublime fusion of passion and peace." - The Radiance Sutras, Tantric Text

Remember what I said earlier? Pleasure is a necessity. It is your birthright. It is the essence of your wild feminine.

Now we come to my favorite topic: sexuality and pleasure. Do you see how they are entwined? How do those words make you feel? What sort of response do you get in your body as I say those words? Excitement, desire, fear, a tightness in your belly? Just notice. Anything and everything is okay. We may all have a different response.

Sexuality is your Shakti. Your wild feminine energy, your Shakti, is your sexual energy. And, remember, your sexual energy and your creative energy are one and the same. This energy is within you. Even if you feel it is lying dormant, it is there. And it is powerful. You thrive on your sexual energy. In all its aspects, it feels way too amazing to just say, "Oh, well, I don't feel sexual anymore and I am okay with that."

Right from the start, I want you to remember that to have amazing sexual energy, you do not have to have a partner and you don't have to be having sex. You need no partner to feel and love and utilize your sexual energy. Your sexuality is yours and yours alone. But you don't want to miss out on the erotic orgasmic energy of your Shakti. Because it is your juice for life, it is your passion for all things. Not just sex. So why would you not want to feel that? And when shared with others it is beautiful, sexy, and wild.

Your sexual energy is your passion—your passion for life, for people, for your creations. Without sexual energy, you cannot create and we all need/want to create. We create art, food, livelihoods. The greatest art you create is your life and your sexual energy gives you the passion to create your best life, no matter your age.

Our sexual energy, our Shakti, keeps us rooted in the pleasures of the moment, whatever they may be. We are present in our bodies. Isn't that the way you want to move through your life—with desire, passion, excitement, curiosity, laughter, trust, exquisite feelings? Your sexual energy allows you to really feel everything in your life. It opens you up to receive, to embrace, whether it is a lover, a creative endeavor, or just daily life itself. It opens you up to find ecstasy in the mundane, to find ecstasy in the everyday ordinary. And isn't that what we all desire?

How is YOUR sexual energy right now? Are you even connected to it? Do you know how your Shakti feels? Not how you think it should feel, or how someone has told you it should feel, but how your very own unique Shakti feels?

Do you know how it feels to be vibrant, alive, yearning, juicy? Your Shakti energy is all of these, and even more. Are you in touch with all of these feelings and emotions or are you sometimes afraid of them?

Without Shakti we become stagnant. We have low energy. We feel no desire to do or feel. Life may seem boring. Our joy of life is diminished. Lack of Shakti may lead to feeling depressed. We see no beauty, no magic in our lives.

When we light up our Shakti and continue stoking her fires, we have a powerful zest and desire and energy for life. We feel the magic. Even better, we know we are the magic. We are connected to our wild feminine power and we know we can create anything. We feel so good and right in our own skin. We love ourselves. We love our bodies. We are comfortable with touch. We own our desires and we are comfortable with them. We know our uniqueness and we own it.

So how do we begin to embrace and stimulate this beautiful energy, this fire? Or, if we already feel comfortable with our sexual energy but want to enrich that energy and use it for our lives, not just for sex, how do we do that?

First, we need to look at our limiting beliefs and attitudes around our own sexual energy. We need to look at how we feel about our bodies and why we feel the way we do. Maybe we look back at how we've felt about and used our sexual energy in the past. Do we even feel comfortable with our sexual energy when we are having sex? How does the idea of sexual energy as your life force—your unique, vital life force—feel to you? Have you blocked yourself from feelings, thoughts related to sex or sexual energy? Have you denied yourself those feelings? Are you ready to rekindle your fire? To rekindle your burning life force, your passion for life? Sit with these questions for a while. Journal about them if you wish. This is still about exploring.

Passion is powerful and, therefore, it can be scary. But passion is why we're here as humans. We have been given this great capacity for desire, for passion.

To feel our sexual energy, we must first be open to it. And that begins with loving our own bodies and being comfortable with them. It begins with knowing what pleasures you, what feels good to you. It means knowing that your body, your yoni, your breasts are sacred centers of knowing and pleasure, knowing that your body is meant to be touched by you. Giving yourself pleasure is one form of self-love. Just getting to know your physical body, your intimate parts, is so powerful.

Do you look at your body regularly? When you bathe, do you touch your body with your hands? Do you touch your body other than just bathing? Can you caress your own breasts? Do you know how they feel? Not in search of a lump, but as a loving self-caress, not even sexual? Do you know what your yoni looks like? What do you call your yoni?

Answering these questions should give you an idea of how comfortable you are with your own body. Maybe at one time you were more comfortable than you are now. Or maybe it is just the reverse. Maybe you became more comfortable with your body as you grew older.

In the "Movement" chapter, we talked about how your body is so amazing just for what it does for you. This is where being comfortable with your naked body begins. Knowing that your body IS amazing. It doesn't have to look a certain way, or be a certain weight, or have less hair or more hair, or be thinner or fatter. It is amazing because it is you! And from this knowing, comes a deep appreciation of your physical body, in all her nudity.

Our wild feminine bodies are receptive. When we begin to express our deep wildness, our bodies desire pleasure. Pleasure of all kinds. Our bodies want to be touched, caressed, massaged. Our bodies desire the pleasure of delicious foods, stimulating vistas, delightful aromas. Our bodies desire sensual and sexual pleasures.

Our deepest desires and wisdom are in our belly and pelvis—the center of our wild feminine essence, our Shakti. As we have come this far in our journeys, our Shakti energy has been building. We have been releasing her a little at a time. Now we are ready to truly honor her and release her in all her wildness. We are ready to give ourselves permission to feel pleasure, to look for pleasure, and to give ourselves pleasure—in whatever ways that feel best to us. Maybe you've been there before and you remember how it feels, or maybe you think you've never really felt that but you are ready to explore, to see what those flames feel like, what your desires will ignite. And, often, that takes a lot of exploring, curiosity, and creativity.

So let's begin, shall we?

First, let's go back to your pleasure list that you made earlier. As you look at it, notice the ones that are purely physical pleasures for your body. You'll begin with these, just so you get used to giving yourself pleasure in small ways. Maybe you have already been doing some of these. If so, do they feel comfortable to you? Do they feel pleasurable?

Before we can give pleasure to our own bodies, we need to feel embodied. Notice how we keep coming back to this word. We want to be in our bodies, noticing, feeling, and being comfortable. Letting our minds quiet. Remember those three or four deep breaths. They are always tools to bring you into your body and settle your mind and allow you to relax.

Sensual body meditation practice—loving your body

Let's begin with those deep breaths. Find a comfy seat where you will not be disturbed and feel free to lie down, if you'd like. You feel quiet and safe and comfortable. Begin by taking a few deep breaths with some long, sighing exhales to settle you into your body. How does your body feel right now? If you sense any tension, especially in your chest or belly, just continue to breathe deeply until you feel yourself letting go of that gripping.

When you feel settled, take your awareness to your breasts. Just notice any sensation you might feel. Notice any thoughts or reactions that come to you. Gently cup your breasts with your hands. Just softly touching and massaging. Just honoring them and giving them love. As you do this, think of the ways your breasts have been there for you. Have they brought you pleasure? Have they nursed babies? Are you proud of them or have you always wished they were different? Just notice what arrives and be there with it. When the time feels right, gently say to your breasts, "Thank you. I love you. To me you are beautiful." And just breathe.

Now move your hands down to your low belly. If you are comfortable with it, gently cup your hands over your yoni or your pubic bone. Just rest them there. What do you feel? Do you feel warmth rising from your pelvis, your yoni? What sensations or feelings are arising within you? Just breathe. Think for a moment about your relationship to your yoni. How has it been? Has it brought you pleasure or discomfort? Or maybe some of both? Just sit and breathe. When it feels right, say to your yoni, "Thank you. You have been through so much with me. I want to honor you. I want to listen to you. I want you to feel safe and pleasured. I love you. You are beautiful and sacred."

Throughout this meditation with your sweet body, use words that resonate with you. Just make sure they are loving words. Because far too often we have criticized our bodies. When we begin to embrace our wild feminine and we begin to listen to her, we want to love and honor her.

As you end this mindfulness with your body, bring one hand to your heart and one hand to your belly. Take another deep breath in gratitude before opening your eyes. If you did the entire meditation with your eyes open, that is great! If this meditation was a struggle for you, if it felt uncomfortable, keep coming back to it. If you don't already, you will begin to feel a great love for your body. And all self-love starts with loving your body just as she is. Self-love starts with appreciation.

Your sexual energy is what makes you feel alive, gives you passion. When we pleasure ourselves, when we enjoy orgasms through our own touch, we take this passion out into the world with us. This orgasmic energy fuels our creativity, it fuels our lives and everything we touch. This orgasmic energy is not only our life force but it is the life force of all creation. That is how powerful it is. And when we give ourselves or allow ourselves to receive this orgasmic energy, we are powerful. We are ecstatic. We are transformed. This is your Shakti, your life force, and nothing, absolutely nothing, is more powerful.

One of the reasons this orgasmic energy is so powerful is because our bodies secrete such powerfully amazing hormones when we orgasm or even when we just feel sexual pleasure. Sexually and sensually touching our bodies produces serotonin, oxytocin, dopamine, etc. A pure cocktail of feel goodness! Through orgasm and touch we feel ecstatic, we feel pleasure, and we also feel connected—connected to ourselves, connected to our partners, if we have them, and even a deeper connection with all creation.

Orgasm has lots of benefits. We know that women who feel good about their sexuality and orgasms are more self-confident. They move through life with more happiness and grace. Orgasms of any kind, and there ARE many different kinds—clitoral, deep vaginal, and total body, just to name a few—improve your immune system. They improve your happiness level. Orgasms enable you to bond with people better and not just the person you had sex with. Orgasms are a great stress reliever. Orgasms lessen depression, help you sleep better. Orgasms increase blood flow to all parts of your brain. And studies show that sexual satisfaction improves with age! So have I told you enough that you are ready to touch yourself or grab a partner? Or maybe at least explore the possibility?

In Tantra, and in embracing our wild feminine Shakti, we believe that sexual energy is sacred. Our bodies are vehicles of pleasure and that pleasure connects us to all things. And to feel that ecstatic pleasure, we begin with relaxation, mindfulness, breath, and touch. Does this sound familiar? It's all about being present, being in the moment. You cannot have a fully ecstatic orgasmic experience without being fully present in your body, and if you are with a partner, fully present with your partner.

Exploration and curiosity are your best friends when it comes to loving your body and knowing what your body likes and wants. It is a shame for a woman not to know what pleases her, what turns her on, what feels good, and not just sexually. Do you really know what you love? Do you really know what turns you on? Those things evolve so it is a constant beautiful learning. And, as I said before, sensuality is a wonderful starting point for discovering what turns you on and what feels good, to your skin, to your senses, to your body, to your spirit. Just as we are all sexual creatures, we are all sensual creatures. But you may have lived so long in your head that you really aren't aware of your senses—what you really love to eat, taste, feel, touch, hear. This is a start to getting turned on, turned on to yourself and turned on to life.

Answer honestly, how many times are you fully present when having sex? Are you fully in the moment? Or are you worrying about how your body looks, or how your body is responding, or thinking about what you need to do afterwards? Does any of that sound familiar?

Amazing sex and great sensuality is about letting go of all those thoughts, of getting out of your head, and just being in ALL the sensations your body is feeling. It is about surrendering and letting go, with yourself or with a partner. To be able to do that we must feel totally comfortable and at home in our own skin. We must believe that our bodies are delicious and deserve to feel pleasure. And we then give them permission to feel pleasure. In fact, we encourage it. It is called desire. One of the most beautiful words in our language.

So I want you, if you don't already, to have this kind of pleasure. Whether with yourself or a partner doesn't matter. I just want you to feel this ecstasy and to take this ecstasy into your life, into the world. Just think what a beautiful place this would be if we were all ecstatically happy because we gave ourselves permission to be! And we sought it out. It doesn't matter how old you are, what size your body is, or how long it has been since you felt this sort of pleasure. It IS available to you. And your wild self desires for you to feel it, to embrace it. I hope just reading this has brought a smile to your face and, hopefully, heat to your body and a desire for touch and pleasure. Remember, touch doesn't have to result in orgasm. Just the pleasure of touch is what we want.

We all, regardless of our ages, deserve to feel and have and use this energy. And once you own your sexual energy, you will know that this powerful energy is always available to you. It is SO much more than just sex. It is also amazingly erotic sexual desires. It is all-encompassing. And oh so worth a little effort to cultivate and become familiar with if you seem to have lost yours.

To live a full, passionate life at any age, we must honor and trust our sexuality. As human beings, we are sexual creatures. Of that there is no doubt. Our divine feminine energy is sexual in nature. It rises from our womb. It is our life force. If you deny your sexuality, or even your sensuality, you are denying your very own life force. This life force that makes you feel alive, drives your actions and desires, gives you pleasure and leads to a life well-lived. So why would you want to deny yourself that? We cannot fully express our humanness and experience our lives to their fullest, without owning and embracing our sexuality.

Owning our sexuality is a huge step in living a passion filled life. We know that when we own our sexuality, we are confident. We are strong. We trust ourselves and our inner knowing. Before we can own our sexuality, we have to learn to love our bodies, trust our bodies, and love ourselves. Sometimes that means we have to first deal with trauma or other sexual issues in our past. And sometimes that requires help from professionals. But often, many women can begin to develop love for their bodies by taking baby steps toward exploring their own bodies, exploring their own feelings about their bodies.

This is what we have been practicing as we moved through this book. Many of our feelings are not ours at all but those of society. We have been told to feel this way; we have been told we should look this way or act this way. Letting go of those old beliefs is where we begin. And a shift in perspective of how you look at yourself, how you look at your body, is a great place to begin. Beginning to tell yourself that you are truly unique, your spirit is unique, and your body is unique. All bodies are unique and all can feel pleasure. We are made to feel pleasure. And our bodies are our tools for pleasure.

I hope that as you have been reading this book, you have taken on some of the practices or rituals and that you are now feeling much more connected to your authentic self. To your deep desires, feelings, and wishes. From this feeling of connectedness comes self-love. Maybe you have begun to treat your body as the beautiful sacred vessel that it is. How does that look for you?

Nude body embodiment and love meditation

In the previous body meditation you touched your breasts and lower belly and/or yoni fully clothed. How was that for you? Did you journal about your feelings?

Now you're going to take that a step further by doing your meditation or body practice in the nude. Just make sure you are in a place where you feel safe and comfortable. Remember, if this feels scary to you, that's why you are here. To find ways to enjoy your own body and adore her. Maybe instead of being fully naked, you prefer to have a soft wrap around you that gives you access to your body. Or maybe you'd be more comfortable just wearing fewer clothes than you usually do—only your bra and/or panties. Whatever feels right to you and, maybe, stretches you out of your comfort zone just a little.

Lie down on your bed or a soft cushion. Settle yourself by taking some deep full breaths all the way into your belly. Long, sighing exhales. Do this until you feel peaceful. Eyes can be open or closed. Continue to feel your breath as you drop into your body. Begin to gently move your body, maybe a stretch or two, maybe just slowly rolling side to side, moving your arms and legs. There is no right or wrong way to move here. Just give your body the freedom to move how it wants. Feel your breath.

As you move, notice if there are places in your body that feel pleasurable. Not necessarily something exceptional, just a sweet feeling. Notice how that feels and stay there awhile. As you keep gently moving your body, notice if there are any other spaces or places that feel pleasurable. Notice that that sensation might be different than the first, but it is pleasurable.

Continue to breathe in a relaxed way. Still lying on your back, place one hand on your low belly and one hand on your heart. As you breathe into these spaces, feel the warmth of your hand on your bare skin. Say some sweet loving words to your body, even just a thank you. If it feels right, begin to make soft small circles on your belly, maybe using both hands. Keep breathing and just feel. Now begin to slowly slide your hands up from your belly, moving over your ribs and eventually touching your breasts. Say something sweet to your body and breasts. Continue to breathe deeply, especially if this feels uncomfortable to you. From here, gently massage your hands over your arms and your thighs. Just exploring the feeling of touch on your body and the feeling of giving love to your own body. Do this for as long as you'd like. You could also massage oil or lotion into your body as you do this. As you finish, bring one hand back to your heart and one hand to your low belly. Tell your body thank you and that you love her and appreciate her.

Maybe you'd like to write your feelings, whatever they were, in your journal. What sensations did you feel? What emotions? If you are not used to touching your own body, this may bring up lots of different emotions. Just be with and embrace all that arises.

Remember, this is just about getting used to touching your body and being comfortable with that touch. If you are already comfortable with that touch, and if this then feels more like a sexual touch moving you toward desire and orgasm, embrace that also. As long as it feels good, go for it.

Sensuality and sexuality begin with loving our own bodies. When we love our bodies for the amazing creatures they are, we feel comfortable in our own skin. And being present in our bodies is a prerequisite for magical sensuality and sex, whether by ourselves or with a partner.

We need to have a relationship, a connection, with these intimate parts of our body. This is difficult for some women. When we have this real connection with the intimate parts of our bodies, we feel comfortable with her, we can touch her, and, more importantly, we can communicate with her. You cannot feel pleasure if you don't even have a relationship, a connection, with yourself and know what you want. Pleasure is healing in body, mind, and spirit. Even if you never want to use this vital energy for sex, you want it for your life.

All of the pleasures in our lives happen when we are fully present. We can only feel real pleasure as it happens in the moment. And we are not able to feel that pleasure if we are stuck in our heads thinking about something else. This is why being in our bodies is vital to a life well lived and a life lived with passion. To feel passion, desire, joy, ecstasy is to be in our bodies and notice those sensations as they build. To become familiar with how these emotions feel in our bodies. And as we build upon these desires, we want more because we feel so connected.

For a few moments, think about the desires of your physical body. What are the ones you know well? Desires of food, water, warmth, etc. Are there desires that you may not be as familiar with? Do you have desires you are uncomfortable with? Why? Do you know what turns you on physically, sexually? Does it scare you to think about what turns you on? Why?

In order to use our feminine sexual energy, our Shakti, we must re-learn what sexual energy feels like in our bodies and then learn to move that sexual energy around. This is a basic Tantric principal. And anyone and everyone can learn to feel and move their sexual energy.

So let's talk a little more about your sexual desires, what feels good, what turns you on. Take a deep breath and let's begin. This will be fun, and pleasurable.

When we talk about sexuality, we're not looking at ways to look desirable to others. There is enough of that in our culture. Most of us have been raised with those ideas. No, we are talking about being desirable to yourself—finding what turns YOU on, what YOUR body finds pleasurable. You are unique and what turns you on may be totally different than what turns me on. And it may not look anything like what you've been told or seen. That is okay. There is nothing wrong with you. All we need is a little exploring of our own bodies, our own sensuality, our own turn-ons. You are not trying to turn someone else on. Later, if you want to turn someone else on, trust me, there is nothing more of a turn-on than a woman who is confident about her body and knows what turns HER on. A woman who desires because she knows who she is and what she wants.

So back to you and your body. What turns you on? Over the next several days or weeks, I invite you to begin an exploration of your own personal turn-ons. When you touch yourself, notice those touches you enjoy most. Which touches arouse you? What kind of touch brings you to orgasm? Keep in mind there may be a variety of touches you enjoy. Read some erotic stories or poetry. Notice the words, the ideas, the stories that turn you on. Watch an erotic movie. What elicits a response from your body? Pay close attention to how your responses feel in your body.

Our turn-ons, those things that arouse us, may change or evolve. This self-exploration, or even exploration with a partner, is on-going. Staying turned on and aroused for most women also requires some novelty, some newness. Different touches or positions may arouse you on different days, depending on your moods. While you are exploring, enjoy all the erotic feelings your body has to share with you.

An easy practice to begin this exploration is through sensuous yoga. I have found, for myself and for many of my students, that yoga is extremely beneficial in getting to know your body and feeling what turns you on. Especially when we approach yoga as a sensual, maybe even a sexual, practice. Giving ourselves permission to move our bodies in sync with our breath and in ways that feel good. Rather than pushing and forcing our poses to look a certain way (that thought is in your head!), just dropping into our bodies and moving in and out of poses fluidly. Feeling fluidity and connectedness with our bodies and breath.

There is a beautiful sensuality to yoga and yoga movement. When we are in our bodies, we begin to notice how sensual we feel as we move. But just like sex, that feeling doesn't happen if we are stuck in our heads. It requires embodiment and relaxation—a softness, an ease that is there, even in strong muscular poses. We bring our wild feminine into the yoga by being receptive, by surrendering to our breath, body, and the movement. And this works even if it is a more masculine energy pose, such as any standing pose. So as we embody our wild feminine we find that joy and sensuality. We begin to relax and enjoy our bodies. This not only brings us to a greater enjoyment of our bodies but is a great teacher for the skills for great sexuality—relaxation and breath and pleasure. They all go together.

If you don't already have a yoga practice, I highly recommend it. Hopefully, if you already have a practice, you have noticed the sensuality in your practice and maybe have seen that translate into your bedroom. And if not, as you go back into your practice, play with your wild feminine on your mat. Remember, she loves to play. She longs to feel sensuous and sexy.

Now let's talk about sensation in your lower body, especially pelvis, hips, and yoni. Many of us have an exceptionally tight abdomen and pelvis and gluteus. When these areas are tight, we usually also find we are continually gripping in our pelvic floors. Your pelvic floor is a huge player in your sexuality. When our bodies are continually tight and gripping in these areas, it is much more difficult to feel pleasurable sensations. Great pleasure and great sex (alone or with a partner) comes with relaxation of your entire body, including your pelvic region. So the first thing we want to do is learn to relax and our breath and body awareness is our greatest tool.

Movement exercise—releasing your pelvic floor for pleasure

This movement meditation is about releasing and letting go. We must learn to release and surrender our muscles before we can learn to use them for sexual pleasure. A strong pelvic floor is easily able to release as well as activate.

You can do this exercise sitting or lying on your back. Until you get used to the feeling of gripping and letting go, it is sometimes easier to notice when lying on your back. Begin to bring your awareness to your breath, just taking a few deep breaths. Can you feel your breath in your belly? Take your attention there. Just slowly begin to scan your belly area, noticing where you might feel a gripping or tightness. Feel your hips in the same way. Notice your glutes. Do the muscles feel engaged and tight? Once you have noticed these sensations, focus your breath and awareness into each tight area. Your long exhales will help your body release tension. With every breath, feel yourself letting go just a little. Feel your body begin to gently soften and let go of its grip. As your low belly and glutes begin to soften, take your awareness deep inside to your pelvic floor, your yoni. See if you can begin to feel a softness, a warmth there. A feeling of your pelvic floor releasing. Stay with your breath in this area as long as you like, allowing more softness and release to come into your body. Feel as if your belly and your yoni are breathing by themselves, feeling the movement of your breath in your lower two chakras—your root chakra and your sacral chakra. Often when we release the gripping of this area, we feel a sense of our bodies sighing with release. It feels really sweet. This is a practice that can and should be done regularly, but especially as you become more aware of it, when you know that you are holding tension and muscular tightness there.

The more we are connected with our pelvises and our yonis, the better we are at listening. Our yonis have a great wisdom and they are powerful. We need to know how to listen to their wisdom. This wisdom in our wombs, our lower bellies, and our yonis is our Shakti, our wild feminine energy. It is an ancient wisdom and when we get in touch with this wisdom, this energy, we are just remembering who we are. You have always been this person. Loving the intimate parts of your body gives you confidence and this ripples out into all your life and relationships. So take a few moments to converse with your yoni. Does she feel alive and juicy? What would make her feel alive and juicy? Talk and feel.

When you are connected to your sensuality, your sexuality, you feel alive, you are juicy and vibrant and confident. And this shows up in every area of your life. You are connected to your essence, to your sexual energy. This field of energy that you exude when you are connected, can be felt by people you come in contact with. They are drawn to you because they feel your vibrancy, your aliveness.

Turning inward to my sensual nature is something I do often. And I have done it for years. Turning inward to my sensual side brings me clarity and calm. Because that is who I am at my essence—a sensual, sexual, feminine creature. And so are you. When I turn inward, I am noticing what pleasure I need to give myself in that moment. What will make me feel good. When I talk pleasure throughout this book, I am talking about pleasures that feed our bodies as well as our spirits. When a pleasure is healthy—whether it be sex, or touch, or food—it lifts our spirits as well as pleases our bodies. It improves our immune systems. Isn't that enough reason to give yourself an orgasm every day?

We are pleasure creatures. We have evolved because of pleasure. Pleasure has so many faces. Pleasure of the body—our sensual pleasures, our sexual pleasures. We take pleasure in tasks completed if those tasks are coming from our true desires. We get much pleasure from helping others, but to keep getting pleasure from helping others we must also give pleasure to ourselves. Fill up our wells, fill up our resources. Otherwise, we become martyrs.

Pleasure is something I give myself every day. It is one of my life's intentions. Because when I feel pleasured in lots of ways, I am content, happy, fulfilled, and, maybe most importantly, I am passionate about everything I do and have. I am passionate about the ones I love.

My nature has always been sensual and sexual. And that has become even more so as I have grown older. I have lived and honored my Shakti, my sexual energy and flow, my entire life. And I am so aware of it that when I feel my sexual energy is low or lacking, I do not feel like myself. That is how vital our sexual energy is. We need to feel it and use it to be our true authentic self. No matter our age. My sexual energy drives my desires for painting and writing and exercising and moving. My sexual energy drives my desires to feel pleasure. My sexual energy drives my desires to share erotic feelings with a partner—to feel and share desire, to feel and share love. My sexual energy drives my desire to take care of myself in all ways, in both my body and my spirit. My sexual energy cannot be separated from who I am. And the few times in my life when it did feel separated, I did not know who I was. I had forgotten but I knew that "I was not me." That is how beautiful and powerful sexual energy is and can be. Trust me. Every woman has that ability, that desire, that power.

Much pleasure for me comes from sex. It always has and I hope it always will. As I have aged, I have found that sex is even more pleasurable. And it makes me so sad to see so many women stating emphatically "I don't want sex" or "I am happy without it." I truly believe they don't know what they are missing and they are afraid to look for it. Because great sex can be had by yourself. And that is where it should start, especially if you've had no interest for a while. Remember, sex is natural. It is natural for everyone, no matter your age, or size, or financial status. I read just the other day that having an orgasm daily is the best thing women can do for their pelvic floor! How wonderful is that! Instead of doing those boring Kegel exercises, you can just give yourself an orgasm! Way more fun, much more pleasurable, and now we know just one of the many benefits.

Sex as mindfulness

Sex is mindfulness. Ever thought of it like that? But it really is. Doesn't that sound like a mindfulness practice you could get into? Great sex can only happen when you are fully in the present moment. And that is great sex with a partner or just great sex with yourself. You must BE THERE! It won't work if you're not. So sex is a great teacher of mindfulness. And it is my favorite mindfulness practice.

Just like any mindfulness practice, you want to breathe deeply and fully. Full mindfulness in sex means you are IN your body. You cannot be in your head and have great sex or even good sex. Same for mindfulness; you must get out of your head and into your body to be mindful and aware.

Mindfulness is awareness of this very moment. And the pleasure of sex comes when you are fully in the moment. Because when you are in this moment you feel the tingle of your skin, you feel the heat as it pours over your body; you feel the soft touch of fingers, your own or your lover's, on your skin; you are your racing heart beat and your quickening breath. To have really great sex, you must be fully embodied. See how we keep coming back to embodiment?

Embodiment is honestly a practice for everything in a really passionate life. I find embodiment to be easiest during sex or lovemaking (use whichever words appeal to you most). Because once I drop into my body, even just a little, I notice even the tiniest pleasure and that helps me to drop in even deeper and to feel more. The more I drop into my body the more I find the most subtle of touches, of feelings, is extremely pleasurable. So that mindfulness, that awareness, during sex grows and expands.

As we begin our sex as mindfulness practice, we focus on subtle sensations first. Just exploring our bodies with soft touches. Doesn't have to be erogenous areas. Anywhere on your body is fine. But I promise that if you stick with me here, you will find that most of your body is erogenous. Isn't that delicious! Most of our bodies, if we're not used to being fully in them, have lost much of their ability to sense subtle sensations. So begin to explore your body with soft touches (fingers, feathers), subtle tastes. Close your eyes and notice soft sounds. This is a good start to learning what turns you on. Let yourself sigh softly and then maybe moan softly. Play with just expressing yourself vocally with non-verbal sounds. And if you start to feel silly or weird, remember you are practicing mindfulness, awareness of the present moment. So it is all worthwhile. And it will begin to bring you much enjoyment. I promise.

Relaxing blissful breath

This breath can be used anytime you wish to relax and soften. Even if just practiced for five or six breaths, you will feel yourself settling into your body and relaxing. I especially recommend it as a prelude to sex or self-pleasuring. To experience the fullest taste of your pleasure, your body must be relaxed and calm. And when you relax and grow calm, you move into your body and out of your head. Pleasure is felt in the present moment and you need to get out of your head and into your body. But you already know that, don't you?

So sit quietly or lie down. Make sure you are warm and comfortable. If it is a prelude to pleasuring yourself, maybe be nude or lightly clothed with soft material. Close your eyes. Take a moment to just notice how you feel in this moment. As you do this, soften your shoulders and relax your jaw, parting your lips.

Begin to breathe in deeply through your nose, feeling the softness of your breath. Hold the breath for just a moment and then exhale through your mouth, long and slow. Continue to slowly breathe this way. No hurry or forcing. After a few moments, begin to let your body make noise with your exhale, maybe a sigh or a moan, whatever your body feels the urge to do. No urgency to any of it, just a feeling of softening, of letting go. This surrendering, or letting go, is felt throughout your body as well as in your head. Your mind and thoughts begin to relax and slow. Continuing to breathe in this manner, notice any sensations in your body, especially your low belly and your pelvis. Continue to breathe like this for as long as you need to feel relaxed and fully in the moment. You want to feel totally embodied. Which might be an odd feeling if you are not used to being there.

Re-sensitizing our bodies

Coming from a culture that loves to live in our heads, we often lose sensitivity in our bodies. And sensitivity is where pleasure comes from. Being sensitive to all the senses—touch, taste, sight, sound, smell. It is easy to begin to sensitize ourselves again to those simple pleasures of feeling in our bodies. This practice, obviously, brings you back into your body and brings you an awareness of the pleasures to be felt just by being in your body.

Choose a time and place where you can be undisturbed. Settle in to a comfortable spot, either sitting or lying down. I like to lie down for just about every practice I have given you that involves pleasure and breath. Just feels more relaxing to me. But you decide what works for you.

Begin with our Relaxing Blissful Breath. Breathing in through your nose and out, long and slow through your mouth. Take at least ten breaths like this. When you feel relaxed, draw your awareness into your body, just noticing any sensations. How is your body feeling at this moment? Not getting caught up in anything, just noticing.

Now begin to gently trace your fingers along your arm. Very, very softly, just the gentlest of touches. How does it feel? Let your skin respond to this soft sensation, this gentle touch. Continuing to move across your upper chest, maybe moving to the other arm and hand. Soft lines or circles. Glide your fingers across your open palm. Continue this soft touching anywhere you can easily access your skin—your belly, legs, feet. You can also gently touch over your clothes. Notice the difference in sensation, if any. Maybe gently glide your fingers over your face and neck. Give yourself permission to let this feel good. It is not a sexual touch. It is just allowing your body to find its way back to the sensitivities it may have lost. These sensitivities are so important to your pleasure.

In addition to using your fingers, you could also try a feather or something else that is soft and creates a light touch. Just like in a yoga practice, you are exploring your body, finding different sensations, seeing what feels good. So just play and experiment. Just looking for the experience of feeling touch and allowing yourself to enjoy that feeling.

Orgasmic breathing

Now let's talk about orgasmic breathing! Sounds more interesting than just regular breathing, doesn't it? We'll practice some tantric breaths and learn to draw that energy up from our yonis and pelvises. This practice is also a wonderful way to warm up your sweet body for sexual play. And it is truly just as easy as breathing, yet so powerful. This is something you can practice as often as you like. As you learn to practice it, you will hear the sound of your breath audibly. But it can also later be practiced in silence, so no one really knows that you are stirring up your sexual energy! How sweet is that? And remember, sexual energy is your passion for everything, especially creativity. It is not just for sex. Sexuality and creativity cannot be separated. True sexual energy and passion for life are one and the same. But remember, you don't have to have sex to have sexual energy and feel it in your life. Though I highly recommend the sex! So let's use it, women!

This breath is used to stir up your Shakti energy and move it through your body. It is a strong, vibrating breath meant to arouse rather than relax. You have already used your breath to relax. Now you learn to use your breath for orgasms and sexual play. This deep orgasmic breath helps keep your arousal high and allows you to feel pleasure longer. It doesn't have to lead to orgasm. But it does cause warmth and stimulation and can be a great start to a powerful orgasm, if you wish.

Find a comfortable place to be alone. This breath can be practiced sitting or lying down. Begin with a couple of deep cleansing breaths, in through your nose and out with a sigh through your mouth. As you follow your breath, begin to feel your body relaxing. Don't hurry it. Just breathe and allow your breathing to deepen and relax you. Relaxation is most important to sexual energy. When ready, take your awareness to your lower belly, your pelvis, and your yoni. Begin breathing through your mouth, both for the inhale and the exhale. As you take your next inhale through your mouth, feel yourself drawing your breath up through your yoni, as if you were sipping through a straw, bringing your breath all the way above your belly button. The inhale through your mouth is audible. As you exhale with a long audible sigh, let that energy flow back down and you will feel a release of your pelvic floor. The inhale breath feels as if it begins with a Kegel and continues pulling that energy all the way up your belly. And your exhale breath relaxes your lower body. Both the inhale breath and the exhale breath are fairly quick, especially as your body gathers momentum and arousal. As you continue with this breath, you will begin to feel a warmth in your yoni and your lower pelvis. You are beginning to feel blood flow in this area, which is what we want. We can't feel if we don't have blood flow to this area. Continue to breathe in this way, just noticing and being aware of all your feelings and sensations. Everything you feel is okay and good. Also, as you breathe, feel free to make sounds if your body wishes to. You want to just relax, feel the warmth growing in your yoni and belly and just explore the sensations. Continue this breath for as long as it feels good to you. Keep in mind that your first few explorations of this breath may feel difficult, physically or emotionally. Just stay with it. Maybe you don't feel anything at all at first. That, too, is okay. The more you practice, the more you will be able to bring blood flow and awareness to this area.

As we make these internal movements that feel a little like Kegels yet are much deeper, we want to make sure there's no gripping. Eventually, we want this to be a deep internal movement that doesn't create tightening of the glutes (your butt) or the abdominals. As you pull this energy upward, you will feel the abdominal muscles engaging gently. Think of it as sipping through a straw. Just remember, you're relaxing here. This energy is felt first in your yoni, around the perineum, between your vagina and your anus. And this energy you are pulling up toward the belly button.

Breathe at a rate that feels good to you. Feel free to explore breathing a little faster in this same manner, if you wish.

When you are ready to stop, just relax your belly and your pelvic floor and let your breathing return to normal, in through the nose and out through the mouth. As you sit with your breath for a few more moments, just be with the sensations in your belly and pelvis and yoni. How do you feel? Do you feel a warmth? A tingling? Does it feel sexual to you? Allow it to be whatever it is.

If you are having sex with a partner, this is a wonderful breath to stimulate and ready your body for sex. In other words, it will usually turn you on, relax you, and bring blood flow to your body which prepares you for pleasure. It is also a breath that can be used during orgasm to bring a deeper, longer lasting orgasm—breathing during orgasm rather than holding your breath at that moment.

You can practice this often until you are able to jump right into that feeling with just a few breaths.

Chapter 16

Eroticism

"Only the united heat of sex and the heart can create ecstasy. I want my eroticism mixed with love." – Anais Nin

How do you feel when you read that word? What sort of feelings or emotions show up in your body with that word? Does it make you smile, maybe feel a little tingly? Does it just make you think of pleasure? Or maybe you belly tightens a little in shame or fear, rather than excitement. In our culture, eroticism is often, and mostly, associated with sex and sometimes porn. Because of this, women often feel scared or ashamed of feeling erotic, or just eroticism in general.

To me, eroticism and sensuality are companions, exquisite companions. We cannot feel either sensual or erotic without fully being in our bodies. As a wildly feminine woman, who lives with the rhythm and cycles of nature, you are also a creature of sensuality and eroticism.

Eroticism IS sexuality and sensuality. Eroticism is inviting those pleasures in. Allowing your body to feel all the pleasures. But eroticism also has a component of your mind. True eroticism requires imagination and creativity. Eroticism often starts in our heads and moves down into the sensations in our bodies. Using our imaginations and our creativity for fantasies that fuel our passion. The more creative and visual we are, the more eroticism we will find in our world. Eroticism, for the creative, visual person can be found in all aspects of life. We looked at ways touch and caress turned our bodies on. Now I want you to think about what turns your mind on in a very sexual way? Eroticism and sexuality work so beautifully together. The perfect arousing partners.

Maybe you begin by making a list of what you already know feels erotic to you. What makes you want to have sex? What makes you feel like a sexy woman?

Remember, erotic for one woman may not be erotic for another. We all have our own "feelings" and thoughts and are also shaped by our backgrounds and cultures. What I want for you is to be able to "own" your own eroticism. Knowing that it is yours alone. Doesn't have to look like any other woman's. It is just as uniquely you as everything else about you.

Some things that might turn you on: thinking about your lover and how his lips feel on your skin; remembering how amazingly hot you felt the last time you self-pleasured; reading about someone else's sexual turn-on that aroused you though you may have never tried that; creating your own fantasy of wild, abandoned sex on the beach. Notice what looks erotic to you. What turns you on just by looking at it. This can change often depending on how aroused we are. I find that sometimes just looking at a man's strong working hands turns me on. I immediately begin to fantasize about those hands on my body. This is what eroticism is. How often do you feel erotic? Know what turns you on sexually and be proud of it.

All of these, and so many other things, can be erotic. And owning your eroticism is powerful and pleasurable. Whether with a partner or not. If you are with a partner, owning your eroticism opens up an entirely new richly satisfying relationship. Because you know what you want, what you like, and you are confident enough to ask for it. You can share your fantasies.

Studies have shown that as women, owning our eroticism builds self-confidence and self-power. We are stronger and more confident. You can see those qualities in a woman who is proud of her eroticism and considers it to be who she is in so many ways. This is her wild feminine.

We must feel safe in our bodies, whole in our bodies, and we must remember that our bodies are wild, that we are wild, that we are made up of earth, water, fire, air, and spirit. We must remember who we are and we are erotic and sensual.

Eros is the thread of pure passion in our lives. It is the inner pulse of everything we love, everything we are passionate about. Eroticism brings aliveness to everything we do, everything we are. Eros is feeling, fantasy, and imagination. It is being in our bodies. It is all about sex and yet it has nothing to do with sex. It's not about gender. It is our ability to open, to feel, to let our wildness out. Eros is primal and it is in everyone, just because we are human. It is our humanness and has been with us since the very beginning. It is our ability to desire just for the sake of desire, to want sex just for the sake of wanting sex.

Eros is always there. But maybe we have buried it, not let it out to play, believing that pleasure—orgasmic pleasure of all kinds—is a bad thing. Maybe we are afraid of fantasy. Or maybe we just haven't used our imagination in such delightful ways as eroticism. In our culture, Eros has been given a bad rap. It's misunderstood. We cloak it, hide it, yet it is so primal, we cannot get away from it. When we try to bury it, it often shows up in unhealthy ways.

But Eros is a delicious part of who we are. Often we women are taught to be ashamed of our eroticism or taught to use it as a tool for manipulation, a commodity. We may not have learned that Eros is luscious. It is for our own pleasure, not a commodity.

When we begin to trust our divine feminine, our Shakti, and allow Eros to bring us even more pleasure, we see how we are meant to be—to live in juiciness and delight in every aspect of our lives.

It is that juiciness, that passion, that fire that motivates us to create. We are drawn to what we want. It doesn't take discipline. When we feel full and ripe we begin to see what we desire, what we need. And the sheer pleasure of it draws us to it, motivates us to make changes.

I seem to have always been acquainted with and drawn by my Eros or Shakti, long before I really knew the words for it. Much of my living has been done in the soft animal of my body, rather than my head. I am guided by and make decisions by feelings. Feelings are how I touch my world and how my world makes the most sense to me.

As a younger person, I learned that though I lived this way and felt this way, it was not in my best interest to share my erotic way of living with others, especially as a woman. Openly saying that I was highly erotic, or that I had many lovers, or even the simple idea that life should be full of pleasures, did not usually bring me praise. So I learned to just enjoy my pleasures but keep silent.

I know that the way I was living was right—that life didn't have to be hard, with a list of rules and regulations and to-dos. Life could be joyous, filled with ease. And yes, there would be sorrows and difficulties—sometimes they would even take priority—but I never had to give up pleasures, even if they might be very small ones. I could and did replenish with pleasure.

We can only be fully alive and have rich, juicy lives when we are present, when we see, hear, touch, taste, and smell everything around us. When we feel passionate and erotic. Being present changes our lives as well as the lives of those we come in contact with, especially those we love. This is why we want to embrace our Eros, our wild softness, our receptivity. Our lives depend on it for richness, for deliciousness, and, even more importantly, for depth—those deep, fulfilling moments that bring richness to our lives.

As we awaken our Shakti, our Eros, our wildness, we begin to feel really alive, all the time. How often do you feel truly alive and vibrant? The key is to drop into our bodies. And embrace our Eros, our sexuality, and our sensuality.

Meditation: Erotic merging of our inner feminine with our inner masculine (Sensual balancing of our Shiva and Shakti)

Choose and play a piece of music that makes you feel sexy, erotic. Lie or sit comfortably. Invite yourself into this place with your breath. Begin by taking a deep inhale and then a long, sweet exhale through your mouth. Settle a little deeper into whatever is supporting you. Once more we will use our vivid imaginations.

Take another deep breath all the way into your belly. As you exhale so slowly through your mouth, let your body make any noise it desires, maybe just a louder sigh or maybe a deep moan.

Continuing to breathe deeply and fully into your belly, your womb, your pelvis, continue to sound whatever your body desires.

Placing your hands on your belly, invite your wild, holy, feminine self to come and play. Rub your belly softly and sensuously as you call to her. She is waiting for you to call to her. She is you and she is playful, erotic, wise, and sometimes chaotic because she is wild and holy.

She moves with the cycles of the moon, sometimes waxing—big, full, wild—sometimes waning, sometimes drawing within, sometimes sad or angry.

She has the qualities of water, fluid, sometimes flowing gently, other times wild and fierce. She is always receptive.

How does she feel in this moment? Embrace this feeling or feelings.

Breathing deeply into your belly, rise from where you are. If it feels right, sway your body. Eyes are closed. Feel your wild, holy self. Dance with her, maybe slowly at first, teasing. Then move as she calls to you, with total abandon. Move your feelings. Receive her eroticism. Feel her heat in your pelvis, your root, your yoni.

Allow her heat to flow through your body as you move. Embrace her fully. Be as wild as you feel. Open yourself up, maybe to new feelings.

Feel fully immersed in your wild feminine as you dance with abandon, eyes closed so you can just feel it all. Give yourself up to her eroticism.

When you are ready, begin to slow your movements, gently, coming eventually to a swaying motion and finally to stillness, your hands on your low belly. Feel your heat.

You are now ready to invite in your inner masculine. Your inner masculine is strong and and powerful and penetrating. He is fire energy. He is Yang energy. He is a giver. You are the receiver. He is eagerly waiting for you, just waiting for your invitation. He desires to merge with you and he knows it is your choice. You are the true creator. And when you merge, life bursts forth.

When you receive him fully, knowing this is what you want, you are so powerful. And his fire stokes your desire. You need his fire to get things done, to create. So begin to seduce him. Dance for him. Tease him, show him that you are receptive. You desire him. You desire life in all its fullness.

Feel the eroticism of your foreplay. He is watching with so much want. Move your belly, enticing him, enchanting him. Imagine touching him and begin to dance together. Whisper, moan, imagine, feel the heat of your energies wanting now to merge. Your desire is breathtaking. Feel your breath quicken, feel his breath on your skin.

He wants to penetrate you now; invite him in; seduction is over; you desire your energies to merge. Feel his penetration through your root chakra, your pelvis, as a column of white light. His column of white light moves all the way up your spine as he penetrates you. Receive it with desire, breathing deeper.

Begin to wrap your wild feminine energy around his column of light, winding around it, beginning at your root, your yoni, like a snake encircling his column. All the way from your root chakra to your crown, feel this merging of your two energies. It is erotic, it is ecstatic, it is life-giving.

This is your life force, your wild feminine merging with your masculine. Embrace it fully. You are just your body, your breath, your energy. Let it flow and feel its radiance through your body. Let it seep out the pores of your skin. Touch, feel, sigh, moan with abandon. Breathe.

When you feel you have been penetrated—you have received, you have fully merged—begin to come back to slower breaths. Feel the satiation in your body. Feel the wholeness of you, the eroticism of your pure self-love.

Beginning to bring yourself slowly back to the sensations around you. As you leave this vision and open your eyes softly, know that you have all the love you need inside yourself and this erotic merging of your feminine and masculine can be repeated whenever you feel the need.

Whenever you wish, this erotic merging can be used to pleasure yourself or used with your partner, feeling the sweet merging of both your energies.

Blessed be. Namaste.

Chapter 17

Nourishing and Nurturing Our Wild Feminine Bodies

> "And I said to my body softly, 'I want to be your friend.' It took a long breath and replied, 'I have been waiting my whole life for this.'" – Nayyirah Waheed

How do you nourish your body, your spirit, your wildness? Those meaningful pleasures that bring you into the present moment, those moments when you are fully inhabiting your body, your skin, this moment?

Before we can give ourselves these pleasures, we must be aware of those things that bring us deep pleasure, that open us up to ourselves and nourish our spirits, our feminine souls. When we do this, we nurture our wildness and we feel free, free to live, to be, to share and support others, free to love ourselves and others unconditionally. I hope to share with you ways to move deep inside yourself, to learn about yourself and what nourishes you.

Being nude—and feeling at home in your body

Ahhhh, being nude. It just feels so good. Are you comfortable wandering around in your own skin and nothing more? Or are you rarely naked for more than a little while? Maybe you take off your clothes to shower and as soon as you dry off, you are back into clothes again. Do you ever take a few minutes when you are changing clothes to just be without clothes for a while, before you put on something else?

Being naked is so freeing. And it requires a good bit of being comfortable in your own skin. Literally. This body and skin that has been with you for so long, how often has it enjoyed the realness of being naked? Remember that pleasure comes when we are living authentically, when we are truly being ourselves. And if we are truly living as our own free spirits, we are comfortable in and love our own skin. And that means we are comfortable being naked. For many of us it means we have a great desire to be naked often. To leave behind the structure of clothes, where appropriate, of course. We love the feeling of freedom, the feeling of air touching our skin. This does not mean our bodies are perfect. Remember, there are no perfect bodies.

But there IS your perfectly-you body. The body that has been with you and given you so many pleasures and wants to give you even more pleasures if you will allow her to. Being able to be nude, even if only for a short time to begin with, shows your body that you love her, that you are not ashamed.

I am not talking about anyone seeing you nude. Though that is certainly great too! I am talking about being able to be naked all by yourself. Maybe even passing by a mirror and being okay with that. In fact, that is a wonderful ritual in itself to make you more comfortable. Stand in front of a full-length mirror, unclothed. Begin by just looking into your own eyes. Say something nice to your body. And then just begin to look at your body. Really look. Not examining it in a critical way, which you may be used to doing. But looking at your body in a loving, nurturing way. Noticing the sweetness of your soft, round belly, your breasts, your legs. Slowly turning around to look at the curve of your buttocks, your shoulders, your back. This is YOUR body. The body that has supported you in so many ways. Embrace her and feel good about how she looks.

If this is difficult for you, please just keep coming back to this ritual. Take it slowly. When you feel your inner critic start to chatter, or you feel ashamed about parts of your body, gently bring yourself back to a positive affirmation or statement about your body. Something that reminds you of all she has done. And thank her. "I remember all those long walks we have taken together. Thank you," or "I remember how you grew my sweet baby," or "Thank you for letting me hold my lover next to me." Remember. Remember the good moments.

You get to choose when you want to be naked, when you feel comfortable being naked. Allow yourself to experience this, especially if it is a new sensation to you. Being naked plays a large part in our sensuality. Let yourself see how it feels. Explore your feelings. Love yourself naked. And keep loving yourself naked.

Some easy self-care practices for getting in touch with and falling in love with your body

- ✷ Lying on the bed (or the floor) and gently stretching with very fluid movement. No particular thoughts of stretching a particular body part. Just think of it as moving your body like water. Close your eyes. Let your body guide you. Notice how you begin to feel pleasure from this movement. Your body feels good.
- ✷ At any time, place your hands on your low belly. Pause. Take five deep breaths into your belly. Feel your breath moving through your belly. Say something sweet to your body, maybe just a thank you for giving you pleasure.
- ✷ At least once a day, stand naked before a mirror. Look into your own eyes. Really look. Breathe. If this feels difficult, stay with your breath. Now look at your body.

All of it. Take in your whole body. Turn around slowly. With a positive lens, see the beauty of your own body. Notice your curves, your belly, your shoulders, your thighs, your yoni. Breathe deeply. And then say thank you to your body, every part of it.

* Sit with a pen and your journal. Take a few deep, full breaths to bring you into your body. Now begin to make a list of all the things you love about your body and why. If this feels difficult, please just stay with it. Start with whatever part of your body feels easiest. List as many beautiful attributes of your body as you can think of and the reasons you are so grateful for those parts of your body. This is a list you can keep coming back to and adding to.
* Write a love letter to your body. This is my favorite and one I have done several times in my life, especially if I was feeling, in any way, that my body was betraying me or I was betraying my body. In this love letter you may wish to have a dialogue with your body. And definitely be appreciative. You can also share fears and anxieties that you have with your body in this letter. As you write, listen to your body's responses. Often, I write my body's response.
* Make a wonderful smelling oil for massaging your body. Using coconut oil or sweet almond oil as a base, add a few drops of your favorite essential oils. Take a warm bath or shower. Pat yourself almost dry. Then begin to slowly and sensuously massage your oil into

your body, little parts of your body at a time. Spend time with each part of your body. Linger. Feel the sensuous touch of your hands and fingers on your skin. Smell the delicious scent of your oil. Think of this as anointing your sacred body. Take your time. As you finish, say a thank you to your body. Say I love you to your body.

* Feed yourself your favorite treat. Make it a sensual food if you can. This is an embodied mindfulness practice. My favorite treat for this is a tree-ripened mango from my front yard. You can substitute fresh strawberries, peaches, cherries, watermelon, apple... the list is endless. But juicy is always good! First, I look closely at the mango, noticing its color variations. I feel the smoothness of its skin. I then slice the mango in half, bringing it up to my nose and smelling the ripeness of the fruit, noticing the bright orange color. By this time, my mouth is watering. And I have already engaged many of my senses (sensual, remember). I slowly bite into the mango, sinking my teeth into its juicy flesh. Oh my. I feel its juices dripping down my chin. I taste its sweetness in my mouth. Juice drips off my fingers and hands and face. I feel as if I am covered in its sweetness. A sensuous, decadent, sweet feeling. And one I partake of often whenever I eat, but especially when I eat something as delicious as a ripe mango. Give it a try and I promise you will love the indulgence and want to do it again. I love to "eat

mangoes naked" (the title of a SARK book) because they are so juicy and decadent. Then take an outdoor shower! Wow, to me that is sensual. And mindful.

* Sleep naked. Feel the sensation of soft sheets on your skin.
* When showering in the morning, choose a soap whose smell is intoxicating to you. I love earthy scents or maybe citrus scents to make me feel alive and energized. Place some liquid or the bar in your hands and begin to lather. Slowly and mindfully rub your hands over your body. This feels best if you use your hands rather than a washcloth. I always use my hands because I can feel the touch of my hands on my body. I want you to notice how it feels to soap up your arms, your breasts, your belly, your yoni, your legs. Drop into your body and feel. This is one of the best mindfulness practices. And a calming, grounding way to start your day. It also brings a gratitude and appreciation for your body. And begins your day with sensuality. So, hopefully, you will carry this sensuality with you throughout your day.
* Make Pleasure Dates with yourself. Do anything that brings you pleasure. And do it by yourself. These can be anything that brings you joy.

Chapter 18

Holding All Our Emotions

> "I want to know if you know how to melt into that fierce heat of living, falling toward the center of your longing."
> – David Whyte

Our wildness is always real and raw and messy. Remember this. Living in our Wild Feminine means that we embrace and hold ALL our emotions. Not either/or but "and." I wanted to share with you how that sometimes looks for me and my life and my writing.

As I sit to write this, I am filled with emotion. Christmas holidays are approaching and what fills my heart and mind most is how much I miss my husband, my daddy, my little Abraham kitty, all of whom I lost this year. This sadness has lain just below my skin for several days, ever so gently touching everything I do.

These feelings remind me that one of the beauties of being human is that we can hold several emotions, even conflicting emotions, at the same time. This is truly a reason for gratitude—we can feel it all—sometimes all at the same time if we give ourselves permission.

So how do we, as our wild feminine selves, honor and move through all these feelings? How do we embrace our sadness and also give ourselves permission to feel joy, to know that even through sadness we will move forward and find joy in unexpected places?

We are gentle with ourselves and we embrace our own bodies warmly. We open our hearts and our bodies to everything life offers. Everything. When we feel and embrace our sadness, listening to where we feel this sadness in our bodies, we know that we are opening our hearts even more. And that is priceless.

We shed tears when we wish and we allow ourselves to smile between our tears. We call upon the support of loving Mother Earth, or Mama Moon, or goddess, or whatever name you give to your Divine. It matters not what we call her. I also find, in times like these, that small rituals of my choosing help me embrace, hold dear, and move through any small thing that tugs at my heart.

At this particular time, I bought three candles, each representing my lost loved one. As I lit them the first time, I told each loved one how much they were loved and missed and asked them to be with me and guide me through the holidays. When all three candles were flickering, I sat with them for a while, shedding some tears but also smiling at beautiful memories. I will light these candles as often as I need or want during the holidays. Doing so brings me peace and makes me feel my loved ones' spirits are close.

I also made a small, special altar with photos of all three along with a couple of tea lights. When I look at this, I can't help but smile at them and feel my capacity once more to hold sadness and sweetness.

These small ways of dealing with our sadness, with our losses, can be done with or for anything. It is a means to acknowledge what we are feeling, to acknowledge and embrace our lives. What are some ways you honor and celebrate your sorrows?

A few months later . . .

I am holding tremendous joy and overwhelming sadness, both in this present moment. Though it is very hard for me to write right now with tears blurring my sight. I feel this is the perfect moment to live and show what I've written about—holding all our emotions knowing many times they are contradictory and it feels awkward.

My lover has just left after a sensual day of lovemaking, relaxing, intimate talk. I'm feeling sweetly satisfied and content, drinking a glass of wine. Decided I needed to write for at least a little while so I turned on my iPad. As it came to life, Photos told me I had a New Memory entitled Through the Years. I hit play on the video. My sweet Dave, who died last year, came to life again in the

Memory. Every photo was a close-up of my then husband and some of the two of us together. The theme song was Tim Halpern's "Something Beautiful." I burst into tears on the second photo. And I could not stop crying as I watched the video twice. Sobbing, not just crying. And yet I had felt so much joy and tenderness just a few moments before with someone else. In some ways, I felt guilty, for absolutely no reason. When I stopped crying, I sat for a moment, reminding myself that it was okay. In fact, it was only human to feel extreme sadness yet also hold joy for someone else. I did not have to feel guilty or feel that I had to choose one emotion or the other. So I didn't. I held them both tenderly as I spent more time just being with them and with myself. Ending with a feeling of gratitude and love of life, still touched by sadness for what ended. As you know, it is powerful when we are able to do that. To hold all of our messy emotions, especially the ones that make us feel bad. Our wild authentic self asks that of us, to hold it all, to love it all. And we grow.

The last drafts of this book took place during the Coronavirus and I felt I must talk about those emotions. Right now, we are in the midst of global anxiety. We are all holding so many deep fears, anxieties, and worries. We are feeling extremely vulnerable because we are being asked to live in the unknown. An unknown that is disrupting lives as we know them. And that is scary. And, I imagine, all of this is one reason I found such extreme emotions today.

Maybe you have felt the same way. Most likely you have felt the same way at some time in your life. We are human.

As we embrace our wild feminine natures, we come back to our groundedness, our centers. And from that place of our knowing, being okay with living in the unknown, we are able to hold all these emotions and not be overwhelmed or immobilized by fear. We can make rational decisions as they are needed. We are not fixated on the "what-ifs" of not-knowing. Often in life we are asked to live in the unknown, the not-knowing. Trusting that we are resilient, that we are strong, and that life (or goddess, or Mama Earth) has our back.

Our world has changed dramatically in the past few days. You can just taste the fear and worry in the air, not to mention the overwhelm. I've not been able to write for a couple of days, just couldn't gather any thoughts together. I have no more classes to teach so I have been learning some new skills—teaching online. Difficult times often call for learning new skills, don't they? If I am honest, rather than learning these new skills, a part of me would like to just sit on the floor and veg. Mindless, or as mindless as possible. And I do know that we need to feel and process all our feelings. So that is what I have tried to do. Feel the fear and overwhelm, process it and not get frozen in it. Often fear leaves us unable to do anything or take any action. It can be immobilizing. But as we feel it and process it we are then able to take action, even if small action, from a place of greater clarity. So that has been my intention.

And it came to me, as I was meditating this morning, that these strange times, these times of never-seen-before chaos, are asking me (and you) to continue to live from my wild feminine. It is imperative in times like this to slow down, to move with less force and effort, to receive as well as give, to be more than do. Our entire country is being asked to do this, and for so, so many it is a very difficult way to live. Because most are used to striving continuously and doing without stopping. We are now being asked to stop for a while. To rest and clarify. This all comes from our feminine energy.

For those of us who have been living this way it is more important now than ever that we stay resting in our wild feminine, that we let her guide us. Because she is the healer, the medicine woman, the person who lives in close connection to nature, the earth, and all her cycles. And we can be that light in this darkness. We can help others learn to feel more compassion, to learn empathy, to see that it is good and well to slow down, to really savor the small things that we all share. Now is the time for the wild feminine energy to lead, to heal. The old Bob Dylan song "The Times They Are a-Changin'" seems so appropriate right now. Yes, the world as we know it is changing. But we all have an opportunity to make our world even better. To hang on to the compassion and caring and empathy that we are seeing all around us now.

Most of all we are being asked to live in the uncertainty. To live with not-knowing. And this might be the purest essence of wild feminine. Being comfortable in the uncomfortableness. We have talked about this. Being in a receptive, surrendering mode to our not-knowing. This doesn't mean giving up by any means. It means we are accepting of what is right now. We are not fighting it or denying it. We accept with clarity and ease (as best we can) that there are many things we do not know right now. No one has any idea exactly how all this will turn out.

The truth is much of our lives we have lived with the unknown. We truly never have had control over our lives. We don't know from one day to the next how our lives will be. We usually don't think that way because most of the time life goes on in its normal fashion. This time it is just right in front of us. No avoiding it. So that makes it seem much scarier. But if we take the time to sit calmly, to breathe deeply, we will begin to see that we are always living with the unknown. Just this can bring us peace and allow us to make better decisions for ourselves and our loved ones and our world with a little more clarity. Decisions made from love rather than fear.

Even in all the unknowns, we do have control over our feelings, our emotions, and our responses. But if we are not careful, we give that control over to others, to the 24-7 media, to negative fearful thoughts. So we must all remain vigilant to remaining in control of our feelings and emotions. Not giving those to someone or something else. Often that means distancing ourselves from constant news sources, maybe even distancing ourselves from certain people. It also means taking as much time as we need to process our own feelings. To be there compassionately for ourselves so that we can bring strength and compassion to our loved ones. We can't be in denial and we cannot sit in fear. Taking quiet time for ourselves, asking for help when we need it are all beautiful ways to cope. And all of this comes from our beautiful wild feminine nature. So please embrace her as we move through all of this. She is wise and knowing within the unknown. Trust her. Trust yourself. We will all get through this together and maybe our world will embrace more empathy and compassion for all.

Seems as if the entire world is being asked to embrace its wild feminine energy. Slowing down, pausing, stopping even, asking us to reflect upon our lives and how we have been spending our time, how we have been treating each other and Mama Earth. These are all good things. We have been made to slow down, to reassess. This is what the divine feminine wants for us and from us.

So how are you taking care of yourself? Your spirit as well as your physical body? In these times of great change, as in any time of change, giving ourselves what we need is so important. Doing those things that lift us up, that bring our vibrational energy higher, that replenish and nourish us. Because from this place we can then find a little clarity, a little hope, and we can share that hope and compassion with others. This is much needed in our world right now and will always be needed.

Making everything sacred especially during scary times

I'd like us to think about how everything we do, see, or say is sacred. Making everything sacred is something I have done for many years as a way of making my everyday life be my practice. When we make everything sacred, we are practicing love, we are practicing connectedness, and we are practicing mindfulness. When we make something sacred, we are fully in the moment. And after a while it becomes a way of life.

So are you finding that in this new normal way of life you are making more things sacred? I hope you are. Rituals help us feel that every day, every act, and every moment can be sacred. And we need these little pieces of sacredness more than ever right now. So what small acts of ritual can you do that connect you to the sacred, that connect you to your feminine? Remember that anything we do throughout the day can be turned into a ritual or a sacred moment. All we need do is bring our full awareness to it and do it with intention. And that intention is whatever you choose, whatever resonates with you at that moment.

Sacred things for me are having a cup of coffee; seeing my fruit trees bud and bloom and change every day; smelling the rain as it touches the earth; being with a loved one, really being with them; even a shower is sacred. What about you? What have you made sacred in your life, especially during these troubled times?

> "Love's greatest gift is its ability to make everything sacred." – Rumi

Candle lighting has always been a way for me to have small rituals throughout my day. During this time, as I am spending much time alone in my house, I find I am lighting candles often as a way to ground and center myself and bring me back into the present moment. Because in this moment, I am well, all is well, and during these trying times I often say to myself, "I am well, I am okay, I feel calm." Repeating this mantra as I take deep breaths. Gazing into the flame of my candle.

A beautiful ritual right now would be to really look into the eyes of someone for whom you are so, so grateful. Someone you cherish. Really look at them and tell them what you love about them, why you are so grateful for them. And if they are not in your home with you, use video chat or FaceTime to look into their eyes.

We need connection now more than ever. And our ways of connecting might have to be different, but we can still deeply connect. So let's not lose touch of that. Who can you reach out to, who do you need to talk to, who can you turn to to lift you up?

Yesterday, a friend called me—actually phoned me rather than texting. She said she just really needed to hear my voice. And you know what? We were on the phone, deeply connecting, for more than an hour. It was such a healing time for both of us. We had been texting back and forth a few times over the past week, but just hearing her voice and being able to connect with the inflection of her voice, to connect with our tears and smiles—because you can hear those in voices—was so beautiful and so healing. Turned my entire day around. So turn to your loved ones and friends. Let them know you care and that you need them also.

Connecting with Mama Earth is a necessity for me. I often lie on the earth and just look up at the sky, feeling the earth's support under my entire body. Drawing her calming energy up into my body and letting any fear or anxiety from my body drop into her. She is so patient and so loving.

I hope that at some point during this chaotic time you found yourself connecting deeply to Mama Earth through bare feet or just lying on the ground. We used to do that a lot as kids, remember? When you connect with Mama Earth, you are connecting with your wildness, your beautiful feminine energy. For Mama Earth is the greatest feminine energy, the mother of all feminine energy. And from her energy, you can be replenished as much and as often as you need. There are no limits.

I hope this practice of connecting with each other and with the earth is one that you will continue as we move forward. This is a time of great transformation and change for all of us, for our world, and we must all be connected to our warm, receiving, compassionate feminine energy in order to move forward.

full moon
fierce wind
raindrops on my skin
mama earth under my bare feet
I am wild, I am holy
I draw down the power of the moon
and draw up the energy of the earth
into my belly
I am blessed, I am blessed

Meditation—the power we do have in troubled times

Let's imagine we're just sitting down to chat. Make yourself comfortable. Maybe you have a cup of coffee or tea or a glass of wine. Just settle in. Let's take a deep full breath together and let's sigh out our exhale, letting our bodies relax just a little. Feel your shoulders soften and your jaw relax. Maybe allow a tiny smile to appear on your face. If your eyes are open, just look around at your space and take a moment to be grateful for what you have, what you see. And keep coming back to your breath.

In these strange times, we often feel fearful and powerless. And that's okay. It is human to feel these emotions. It is part of that sweet ache of being human. But right now, in this moment, I want us to remember the power we do have.

— You have the power of words. Our words can bring magic or despair. You have the power to choose your words, the words you tell yourself and the words you share with others. What words have you been choosing lately?

— You have the power to find stillness. To just sit quietly, to just breathe, to just wait. And you have the power to choose to do things you love. You may have to be a little creative right now, but you can still choose to do things that bring you joy and happiness.

— You have the power to drop deep into your body and, from that groundedness in your body, know with certainty that you have been in darkness before and you have emerged. You know that you will do it again. You know you are resilient.

I hope you are staying close to your breath, feeling every inhale and exhale.

— You have the power to put your bare feet on the earth, dig your hands into the dirt, and gaze up at the moon. To feel your connection to all that is.

— You have the power to be wild and fierce and holy. No one and nothing can take that power from you. It is always yours.

As you begin to deepen your breath and think of getting up and going about your day, what will you choose today? How will you use your powers? How will you share with others? Take a moment to bring one hand to your heart and one hand to your belly. What powers can you feel in this moment? What powers might you use today?

Still resting in your heart and belly, what can you be grateful for in this very moment? What is right in front of you that you can feel gratitude for? Sometimes the smallest things can bring such warmth to our bodies, to our hearts. Take a moment to feel your gratitude. Your gratitude brings you power.

Then begin to slowly and sensually stretch your body. Long and slow, moving as your body desires. And, eventually, when you are ready, take another deep long breath and go back to your day.

Blessed Be and Namaste

I wish for you . . .
vivid, brilliant sunrises and glowing sunsets
hot cocoa on a cold, rainy afternoon, maybe with a little Bailey's
down comforters and soft chenille throws
a furry cat to tickle your skin
a dog's lapping tongue to wake you up
Sangria in a glass pitcher with lots of ice cubes, oranges, lemons, and limes and a gorgeous glass to drink it in
ocean waves lapping at your toes
sand crabs scurrying by you on the beach
treasures discarded by the ocean
short, fat candles with sumptuous smells
ruffled skirts and skimpy tank tops
fresh from the oven, gooey, chocolate chip cookies
steamy mugs of coffee (or tea)
art that speaks to you in hushed whispers
art that screams at you
books, books, books with dog-eared pages, broken spines, and love scattered throughout the pages
a slinky red dress that you just love to wear
love letters
outrageous adventures
passionate sex
romantic evenings for one
romantic evenings for two
picnics in Paris (or in your bed)

wine and cheese, wine and cheese, and more wine and cheese

strawberries dipped in chocolate shared with someone special

erotic fantasies that incite your fire

the company of cherished friends and family

your own tropical, pleasure island (imagined is fine!)

outdoor showers for two

walks in the summer rains

long, lazy afternoons

your loved one's voice

hammocks and palm trees or giant redwoods and deep forests, if you prefer

cherished memories

the laughter and wonder of children amidst the storms of life

the sacred joy of knowing that you have a guardian angel (or many) when you've lost a loved one

Wild feminine is (to me)

What does "wild" mean to me? Sometimes when we think of wild, we imagine chaos, things that are unruly and irrational, or living in the wilderness, self-sufficient, without civilization. All of these can be true. But when I use the word wild, as in wild feminine, this is what it means to me.

Wild means I am in touch with all my inner resources, all those parts of me that make me wholly me and holy me.

Wild means I live in tune with Mama Earth, Mama Moon, and all of nature.

Wild means that I remember my ancient roots, my ancient self. I remember all the women who came before me and support me now on my journey.

Wild is loving to be alone with myself, more than just comfortable with myself. Wild is constantly needing to get in touch with myself and my feelings.

Wild is feeling and honoring all my emotions, especially those that society deems unruly, messy, or even wrong. Wild is appreciating them all and knowing that I am all of that and yet I am even so much more.

Wild is FEELING in capital letters. Always being in touch with how I feel, what feelings someone or something elicits in me. Wild is honoring those feelings, diving deep into them, exploring and excavating.

Wild is trusting in myself fully, in my thoughts, feelings, ideas, emotions. Trusting in my body's great wisdom and knowing that there is none greater.

Wild is being aware of my own divinity, my own holiness, and knowing that others are holy and divine in their own right.

Wild is loving my body, honoring her and giving her pleasure. Wild is sharing my body with those I choose and no guilt or shame in the pleasures of my body. The pleasures of my body are sacred.

Wild is living moment by moment, embracing each moment with passion and the energy of aliveness, even the hardest moments.

Wild is living my life to its fullest, its most passionate. Wild is moving to my own beat and allowing others to find their own beat.

Wild is living in the not-knowing, living in the uncertainty, and finding peace and often even pleasure in that uncertainty, because there is a deep intuitive trust that everything is going as it should.

Wild is intuitive living, living from my body's senses, trusting those senses.

Wild is not looking outward for the answers but looking inward.

Wild is taking the time to look inside, to explore my inner workings and feelings.

Wild is being creative, creating a life well-lived, writing, painting, drawing, moving my body.

Wild is being a fully sensual creature and living a fully sensual life. Wild is embodiment.

Wild is touch, touch, and more touch. Touching myself, touching others, touching the world, touching nature.

Wild is joy, choosing joy, and trusting in joy.

Wild is loving the darkness, knowing that growth happens in the darkness. Magic happens in the darkness.

Wild is magic, believing in magic, practicing magic, living and loving with magic, magic in the everyday.

Wild is receiving and asking for what I need. It is also just opening to receive all the abundance and bounty of the universe. Wild is opening to receive my life, opening to receive its wisdom.

Wild is finding that sweet ease within everything, making magic happen without effort, allowing ease to pull me forward without pushing. Because when I choose joy and pleasure then everything I move toward, any effort that I put forth to accomplish what I want, always feels like ease, like sweetness, because I have chosen joy and pleasure. I am moving toward my heart's desires.

Wild is sexy, passionate, creative, sometimes crazy, joyful, sadness, trusting, remembering, pleasuring, receiving, honoring, touching, feeling, darkness, light, fluid as water, ease, graceful, caring, compassionate, loving, orgasmic, untamed, unapologetic, fierce, earthy, grounded, transcending, moonlit, radiant.

How does wild look to you? If you are living wildly, how are you living? What can you do to bring more wild into your life? How can you trust yourself more? How can you love your body more?

Juicy

A good mantra for everyday use and to feel grounded is "I am grounded in pleasure."

That just sounds juicy, doesn't it? It is my hope that many of the practices and ideas I have shared with you are beginning to make you feel juicy and delicious in body and spirit. I find that if my body feels juicy then my spirit also feels juicy and the opposite is also true. Sometimes, just thinking those words—juicy, delicious, succulent, vibrant, sumptuous, decadent, joyful—makes me begin to feel that way. They are words that lift our energetic field to a higher level and often just saying them brings a delicious feeling to my body and spirit. I hope you also find that to be true.

Because that is really what living and embracing the joy of our wild feminine nature is about. When we live in our wild authentic self, making choices from that place, we are living in our highest energy. We feel juicy and joyful and decadent. Doesn't mean we won't also feel into the depths of our being at times too, but in its own way the depths of our being, our sadness, our sorrow, is still a feeling of juiciness, a true feeling of our rawness, our aliveness. We want it all. This is how we live a rich, full, juicy, passionate life. We are open to all of it. In fact we WANT all of it because this is life and we want to be with it. We want to feel it in our bones and marrow. Nothing about our lives is superficial when we embrace our wildness. When we embrace our wildness, we embrace our depth. We embrace our shadows. The more we live that way, the more we want it. We desire it. It is the only way we can truly feel alive. And we are so grateful for that feeling

Life is rich, raw, and messy. Often complicated and chaotic. Beautiful and harrowing at the same time. Filled with ecstatic moments and plunges into the depths. And sometimes just a serene calm. And we crave all of it. We want to love fiercely and freely and this includes ourselves. It must. We want to feel that tingling of passion in our skin, that flowing of energy through our bodies. We want to feel our beautifully wild, passionate Shakti. She is our aliveness.

Conclusion

Make your path to the wild feminine your own. Every woman's path is different and that is a beautiful thing. We are all unique and our wild feminine selves are unique. Mine is not yours. So it makes sense that our journeys to embrace her will look differently.

I hope this book will be a resource for you to begin to explore your own path. I have offered you rituals, ideas, methods, and meditations that I have used. It is my hope that you will read them, see what resonates with you, maybe try several or all of them and then keep only what speaks to you. Because if it doesn't speak to you, you may not continue on your journey to embracing your wild feminine.

It is important to approach any new path with an open mind and an open heart, eager to explore new ideas or actions. Try them a few times, be curious. And then, if they still don't resonate with you, leave them. Move on to another one.

As you begin to choose the ones that speak to you, you will find your own path developing. And remember, our paths are winding and cyclical, which is the feminine way. We are cyclical beings so we cannot expect our journeys to be the same. We will circle around time and time again, sometimes experiencing something new and urgent, often feeling or confronting the same feelings. All of it is perfectly imperfect, happening just as it should.

And the beautiful thing is that as we change over time, our practices will evolve and change. Our own feminine spiritual paths never stay the same or they may become stagnant. So welcome change and newness into your practice as it seems right. Your authentic wild self will not guide you astray. Instead she's always leading you deeper inward, revealing more and more of "yourself" to you.

Our practices, our lives, with our wild feminine self, are fluid and flowing, for she is the embodiment of water. So invite yourself to flow with her, to flow with your rituals and practices, and in that you will flow with your life.

That flow, that ease, is what we're searching for. Notice how good it feels. What it means with regard to our spiritual movements is to not become rigid. Rigidity causes stagnation. When we rigidly hold on to something that may not be working for us, we find we don't go deeper. We don't move forward. We don't get the feeling of fluidity.

Embracing Your Wild Feminine

Most of all, your practices should bring you joy and feelings of happiness. They should never be "have-to." Most of us have enough of those. Play with your practices. Lighten up with your life. Our wild feminine desires pleasure, movement, rawness.

Our wild feminine is also deeply earthy. She is part of the deep earth and always has been. Earthy is raw and real, often messy. She is the womb from which everything originates. She is the maiden, the mother, and the crone. She is sometimes wild, sometimes serene. She is always "home," just as your wild feminine self, your body, is always "home." You don't have to look anywhere else. You don't even have to go outside yourself to find your home, to be at home.

Take what you find in my words and use what feels right to you. And then add on to your practices with other ways that make you feel wild and free, filled with earth and water and fire and air. Evolve, roam, be curious, explore. The more you open your heart and body, the more your wild feminine spirit will guide you and lead you with her desires. She wants to be embraced. And all along the way, feel. How do you feel? What do you feel? Be led by your heart and body.

Journal prompts:

* How do I see my wild divine feminine?
* Can I describe her? How would she describe herself to me?

* How does being authentic and free look to me right now?

The main thing I hope you take away from all this is that there is no one path to awakening and embracing your wild feminine self. All paths will look different. Just as all our feminine wild selves are unique. You may have to try several different things to feel what works for you. However you get there, you will find that it is so worth the journey. And even when we find our wildness and we begin to live fully with our Shakti energy, we are always on that journey, that journey of embracing more wildness, being fully present in our bodies, knowing what turns us on. It is never-ending. And that is sweet. So I hope you'll be curious, you will explore how YOU feel, and you will be creative as you make your path. Take only what resonates with you from this book and even then make it fully, uniquely yours. And if, in the end, you discard all of what I've said, that's okay too. Finding your own way to your wildness, your divine feminine, is all that matters. Because when you truly find your own unique wildness, you will know it. You will feel rich, sensuous, wild, and free in your body and your spirit. You will have a passion for life that you have never felt before. That's my wish for you.

people say you're always so happy, so positive
though I am filled with joy most of the time
sometimes I fall into my depths

there . . . I face my sadness, my fears, and try to gently move myself
through it all, feeling all my darkness
sometimes feeding off it
I love this feeling of raw

and it is you that I trust to see me in these depths, this darkness
it is you that I trust to guide me through
when I need you to

it is you who holds me in your arms
whispering it will be okay
it is you who can chase away my demons
and love me anyway, or maybe because of

just before dawn
soft breeze caressing my skin
warm earth beneath bare feet
moon sliver visible in the indigo sky
today
may I create passionately
may I live wildly and truthfully
may I breathe in joy
and may I soften in grace

home is where I don't have to BE anything, I can just be
home is where I let my hair down and play
home is where I can be my true self
home is anywhere and anyplace I can take a
deep full breath
take a deep breath with me now
I invite you home

home is where I enjoy pleasure with abandon
home is where mistakes are welcome
home is where I find the courage to go on
home is anywhere and anytime I can take a
deep full breath
I invite you home

home is where I am wild and free
home is where I face my darkness
home is where I am grateful for all of it—
joy, desire, sadness, pain
home is where I am grateful for just being human

home is anywhere and anyplace I can take a
deep full breath
home is my body, home is my wild feminine
my body, my spirit, my wildness invites me home
your body, your spirit, your wildness invites you home

when we slow down we are able to feel that sweet softness, that wild yearning
that is inside of us
that wild yearning that's half awake, half asleep
that wild yearning that wants to reach out, so ready to smile and touch and feel
that wild yearning so raw and messy, so beautiful and real
that wild yearning so wanting to feel free
free to love, free to just be in all her wildness
free to just let go and breathe
so today, let's embrace our wild yearning
and live with vulnerability and a heart burst open

breathe
breathe deeply
into your fingers and toes
breathe
into your belly
touch its softness
breathe and know
know you are perfect
breathe
into your yoni
touch its softness
breathe and know
know you are
wild and holy
no one can tame you
breathe
know you are daughter
of earth and moon

wild and turbulent
the ocean, yet
sometimes
I am the contradiction
serene on the surface
wild in my depths
sometimes
the wild is passion, heat
sometimes rage, fierceness
the wild is bringing me to my knees
but you never see that
I fall to my knees
inside my skin, my bones
no one knows, no one hears
I've been brought
to my knees in despair, yet
always, to rise again

good morning
take a deep breath
deliciously wiggle your fingers, toes
let a sigh softly leave your body
ahhhhh
breathe in, find a smile in your heart
breathe in, feel your smile pulse
throughout your body
awakening every part
breathe in softness to find a
joyful ease in your day
breathe in courage
to be authentically you, unique
breathe in courage to live from your heart

deep, deep inside
you are wild and holy and fierce
you are raw and real
deep inside
maybe you've forgotten
but
your body remembers

I dance with the tides
of the moon
I am wild

breathe in
know you are wild
breathe out
know you are holy
breathe in
know you are woman, seductress, healer, poet
feel the rhythm
pulsing in your bones
in your marrow—it has been there since the beginning
breathe in
feel your heat rising from within
breathe out
burn with your passion
dance wild, make love fiercely,
sweat, moan, scream, feel

Acknowledgments

I wish to thank ...

All my students and clients. You have given me more than you can ever imagine and I am so grateful for each and every one of you.

My beta readers: Ginger Fout, Dr. Diana Sinisterra Lores, and Denise Ferrara. Your feedback and enthusiasm were invaluable! Y'all were amazing and I can't thank you enough.

My student, Deborah Paiva (author of *Heal Your Heartache*), for answering questions and offering encouragement, along with lots of laughter, when I needed it.

My editor, Nanette Littlestone, for her expertise and patience in guiding me through this process of writing and publishing. She was a joy to work with and I could not have done it without her.

My mama and daddy for teaching me the juiciness of books at an early age.

Cheryl Moates (author of *You Can Heal Your Gut*), my sister, who inspired me to finish my book when she published her first book! I am so proud of you, Cheryl!

My sweet family. You have always been there for me, loving me, holding me up when needed and sharing so much love and laughter. I love y'all.

Johnny, for loving my wildness.

Additional Resources

1. *Love, Sex, and Awakening* by Margot Anand
2. *Vagina, A New Biography* by Naomi Wolf
3. *Tantra, The Supreme Understanding* by Osho
4. AwakeningShakti.com, Lisa Schrader
5. Caroline Muir, Tantra educator, Conversations with Caroline, YouTube, DivineFeminine.com

Meditations

If you're interested in receiving free audio recordings of the meditations, please contact the author at JoyBreatheYoga@gmail.com

www.ingramcontent.com/pod-product-compliance
Lightning Source LLC
LaVergne TN
LVHW051515070426
835507LV00023B/3121